THE SUNDAY TIMES

BUSINESS ENTERPRISE GUIDE

Forming a Limited Company

8TH EDITION

PATRICIA CLAYTON

KOGAN PAGE

Acknowledgement

The forms are Crown copyright and are reproduced with the permission of the Controller of The Stationery Office.

The author acknowledges the kind assistance of Companies House, Cardiff, in the preparation of this book.

While every care has been taken to ensure the accuracy of this work, no responsibility for loss occasioned to any person acting or refraining from action as a result of any statement in it can be accepted by the author or publisher.

First published in Great Britain in 1990
Second edition 1991
Third edition 1992, reprinted with revisions 1993
Fourth edition 1994, reprinted with revisions 1995
Fifth edition 1996
Sixth edition 1998
Seventh edition 2001
Eighth edition published in 2004

Kogan Page Limited
120 Pentonville Road
London N1 9JN
United Kingdom
www.kogan-page.co.uk

The views expressed in this book are those of the author, and are not necessarily the same as those of Times Newspapers Ltd.

British Library Cataloguing in Publication Data

A CIP record for this book is available from the British Library.

ISBN 0 7494 4150 X

Typeset by Jean Cussons Typesetting, Diss, Norfolk
Printed and bound in Great Britain by Cambrian Printers Ltd, Aberystwyth, Wales

Your calls, answered by your secretaries, in our call centre.

alldayPA will make your small business "sound and feel" like a much larger company.

It makes you more professional and more credible to your new customers.

alldayPA is a live, 24-hour receptionist and secretary who answers your calls, takes your messages, types your emails, sends your faxes, stops the calls you don't want and forwards the ones you do - exactly what a secretary would do if she was there in person.

- **Pay per Call or Pay per Minute**
- **Receive your messages by email or SMS text**
- **Free 0845 number**
- **Same-hour activation**
- **24-hour call answering**

Call now:
0845 057 4000
www.alldayPA.com

alldayPA ™
Your 24 hour Personal Assistant

What We Do

alldayPA is a 24-hour, professional, call handing and message-taking service totally tailor-made for your business.

Real people, based in our UK call centre, answer your calls when and how you want them.

Your PA can screen your calls, stop the ones you don't want, transfer the ones you do, take your messages – everything a real secretary would do if she were sat in your office – but for a fraction of the cost.

Our experienced and professional PA's will impress your callers and enhance your image. They are friendly, dedicated to you and have undergone some tough secretarial exams to ensure they provide the most professional service to you.

Use alldayPA as

1) Receptionist – take calls and messages
2) Switchboard – transferring calls
3) Overflow call handling – when your line's engaged
4) Secretary – diary and typing
5) Holiday cover – when you're away
6) Sales – take your orders
7) Customer Services – manage your applications

How We Do It

We can do as much or as little as you need us to do.

Receptionist

alldayPA will take your calls and messages when you're in meetings, on the road, with a customer, or simply need some time to yourself. All your messages will drop instantly into your Inbox and if selected sent to your mobile by SMS text.

Secretary

Use your alldayPA to type your urgent emails while you're out of the office. Your PA can also manage your diary with our unique online diary function within the free website we provide.

Virtual Switchboard

Let alldayPA handle all your staff's calls, transferring them through or taking messages when needed, therefore avoiding the expense, the training, and the management of your own switchboard.

Call Screening

Avoid the calls you don't want and take the ones you do. All your messages will drop instantly into your Inbox and if selected sent to your mobile by SMS text.

Overflow Calls

Set up your business line so that unanswered or engaged calls are immediately diverted to alldayPA – you'll never miss another call.

Advertising Response

alldayPA can handle many inbound calls at one time and will precisely collate full customer details, take telephone orders or requests for your brochures – even ask where they saw your advertisement for your own campaign analysis.

Emergency Call Out

Have your clients call your 'Emergency Call Out Hotline' and let us handle the emergency quickly and to your exact instructions. We can then contact your back up team at any time or the day or night.

Holiday/Sick Cover

Having 24-hour call handling support behind your business becomes invaluable when a key member of staff calls in sick or goes on holiday. Your alldayPA account stays active (even if you don't use it so often) and takes calls whenever you need it to – you control it.

Order-Taking

alldayPA can be a live, professional order-taking and sales service uniquely tailor-made for your online business. We are available all day and all night to act as your own sales staff and take your telephone orders.

How It Works

When you register you receive your own telephone number.

Choose between:
- 0845 lo-call rate number
- 0207 Central London number
- 0208 Greater London number
- 0113 Leeds number
- 0121 Birmingham number
- 0141 Glasgow number
- 0151 Liverpool number
- 0161 Manchester number

Your number is activated immediately and ready to use.

The call is answered using the tailored script we agree with you when you set up and your caller is completely unaware that the call is anywhere other than at your office.

It's as simple as that.

How You Can Use It

When you get your alldayPA number, you can publish it on your website, your marketing literature and business cards OR ...

You can divert your existing telephone line to it.

All you need for this is a call diversion facility on your landline and/or mobile.

All this means you can use alldayPA full-time ... to answer and transfer all your calls
OR
You can use alldayPA part-time... to answer and transfer calls when you needs us to.

Switch us on or off when you want to.

Why Choose alldayPA?

Nine reasons why you should choose alldayPA:
1) No more engaged tones for your customers
2) No time wasting on unwanted calls
3) No office rental, furniture costs or IT equipment costs
4) No long-term employment contracts
5) No answer-machine to irritate your callers
6) No software installation – easy set up
7) We never go on holiday or take time off sick
8) We offer the most competitive pricing in the market
9) It'll give you more time in your day and give your business more credibility

Corporates

Do you need staff to manage your phones?

alldayPA provide seamless call answering services to Corporates who are looking to outsource call centre functions.

Corporate clients currently use alldayPA for:
- Advertising campaign response lines
- Recruitment hotlines
- First line helpdesk support
- Data input for application or registration forms
- Virtual switchboard

We swiftly implement bespoke services for corporate clients requiring unique processes for their calls, for any purpose, using state of the art telecoms technology.

Call us – 0845 056 1234 or www.alldayPA.com and we'll quote on a competitive package uniquely for your needs.

Right people, right job

Jobcentre Plus can help with all your recruitment needs, at all stages of your business growth. We can help you find the right people to fill your vacancies, at the times to suit your business.

There are many services we can offer you, including:

- Display of your vacancies locally, nationally and elsewhere in Europe*
- Employer suites and interview facilities in many of our offices; and
- Advice on recruitment through a dedicated vacancy service manager.

* countries who form the European Economic Area (EEA) and Switzerland.

All this and it only takes one call, remember the number!

Call **Employer Direct** now on
0845 601 2001**

A textphone service is available for people with speech or hearing impairments on
0845 601 2002

www.jobcentreplus.gov.uk/ employers

jobcentreplus

Part of the Department
for Work and Pensions

**Opening hours 8am - 8pm Monday to Friday; 10am - 4pm Saturday.
Calls charged at local rates.

@UK PLC® a one stop shop for setting up and growing your company

Setting up your company

@UK PLC® has revolutionised the process of setting up a company and getting it trading. **You can now get a company formed today, and have it trading by the end of the week for less than £50**. Over 30,000 businesses have taken advantage of @UK PLC® services and the number joining is increasing by thousands every month.

@UK PLC® was set up to allow small companies to compete with large businesses on a level playing field. It has invested heavily in making it as quick and easy as possible to set up your company and get it trading.

Traditionally you had to go through an accountant or solicitor to get your company formed. This process cost hundreds of pounds and could take weeks. @UK PLC® forms a company the same day, with your choice of name for only **£34.99** – a staggering improvement in speed and quality. Bundled free of charge with company formation is a starter website (SiteGenerator ALPHA, normally worth £24). This gets your company promoted on the web immediately.

Graham Bell, the World Cup Ski racer who graduated to commentating for Ski Sunday sums up the service nicely. Graham formed his company Cloche UK ltd on 22nd August. He took over £ 4,000 on line in September. You can see Graham's site at http://www.skiersedge.co.uk.

The cost to Graham was £42.50 for Company Formation with a paper certificate, £74 for a website upgrade to a SiteGenerator 5LIVE site with full ecommerce, and £125 to Barclays ePDQ for credit-card setup. He pays £24 per month to Barclays for credit-card acceptance. The @UK PLC® package includes hosting, a templated website with online editing, and a full shopping basket with online payment facilities.

Rapid setup and trading is exactly what company founder Ronald Duncan was seeking when @UK PLC® was established. He states:

> "We have made it **quick and easy** to set up
> a company and trade online. The proof is in the number of
> clients that are joining @UK PLC®. Over three thousand
> are joining each month and the rate is accelerating".

Growing your company

Having founded a business, now you need to prosper and grow. Online commerce is expanding at over 110% pa. @UK PLC® clients are at the forefront of this growth.

"Red Shark" started off as a small Northumberland company. It is now the largest online seller of inkjet cartridges based in the UK. It has three UK stores, a US store and two European stores, all of them profitable. Red Shark has gained over 120 local authority accounts through their websites. They are still doubling in size every five months, with a turnover now measured in millions.

Because of @UK PLC®'s success, they are now working extensively within the Public Sector ensuring that suppliers are ecommerced and ready for 2005, when public sector organisations have a requirement to purchase goods and services online. This affects over one million companies. If you trade with the public sector (or plan to) you will be required to have an ecommerced web site which can interact with public sector finance systems. **The public sector market is worth over £25 billion** annually. Even a basic @UK PLC® web site will give you a presence within this market. http://www.bristolebusiness.net is just one example of how @UK PLC® is working with a local council to provide their suppliers with online trading facilities.

@UK PLC® is also partnered with Sage PLC, the largest provider of accounting software to small and medium sized businesses. The two companies have integrated the @UK PLC® web building and ecommerce software with Sage Line 50, the most popular accounting package in the UK, giving you a fully integrated web and accounting system.

@UK PLC® is focused on helping small and medium sized businesses to grow and prosper. Company formation is just the beginning of a relationship, which can span advice and guidance, company secretarial services, accountancy, web services and access to information on government and  large corporate tenders. Through @UK PLC®'s relationship with the business support community of Business Links and Learn Direct, you can be put in touch with an appropriate advisor if you need advice or training. Many of these courses are free and can be accessed online.

Join the @UK PLC® community and start building your business.

http://www.ukplc.net
Telephone: 0118 963 7000

Contents

transactions: preferences and transactions at an undervalue
126; Dissolution in compulsory winding up 126; Restriction on
use of the company name 127

Forming a limited company can be a complex and tortuous business if you are not experienced or too busy. It is best left to experts you can trust to provide you with a new company ready to trade quickly and efficiently.

But mistakes can be costly and awkward, so it is important to buy from specialists who have been supplying thousands of companies to leading firms of accountants and solicitors nationwide for many years.

The leading name in the UK company formations industry for well over 25 years is Stanley Davis.

Stanley Davis started in company formations 40 years ago, set up his own company in 1977 and built it into the best-known name in the business.

Despite having a low personal profile in the industry after selling the successful business to Robert Maxwell in 1988, "retiring", then creating the highly successful Independent Registrars share registration service before selling to Capita in 2000, Stanley Davis, along with the Stanley Davis Group and Sdg, has been widely known and synonymous with Company formations for many years.

Now Stanley is active again in company formations as Chairman of the Stanley Davis Group with a new management team led by Chief Executive Andrew Davis. Andrew not only grew up with the business, he also understands the needs of the market having trained as a Chartered Accountant and gained an MBA from Manchester Business School, then worked in management consultancy before six years at American Express Corporate Services.

Whatever type of company you want, wherever you want it registered, whatever level of formation service you require, the Stanley Davis Group can advise, support and arrange it for you.

Now the best company formation service can set up and establish a new company within minutes at the most competitive prices.

The Stanley Davis Group's eformations, launched in May 2003, is a revolutionary way of forming companies on-line from as little as £30. This is the lowest price on the market yet it is offered by one of the industry's most well-known and respected names, a symbol of excellent customer service and technical expertise.

It is remarkably easy to use. There is no software to download – you simply log on to the website, www.stanleydavis.co.uk, enter the required information and a Certificate of Incorporation is e-mailed back to you within 24 hours.

Typically the time spent forming a company by this route is 5 minutes and the documents are filed with Companies House within a day. With the traditional method it took 40 minutes and typically 16 days to file.

No more signatures are required – all forms are completed electronically. So there is no need to send forms to clients and back again, which makes the whole process extremely quick.

Items such as Memorandum and Articles of Association, registers and seals can be ordered separately and there is no minimum order.

Buyers can pay by credit card or set up an account, which gives the advantage of being able to save data where companies have common officers. Once the order form has been completed and details submitted, a confirmation of receipt will be sent. The Certificate of Incorporation is e-mailed as soon as it is received. The company is then ready to trade!

The company formations business, and the needs of customers have been changing fast. Many new and inexperienced suppliers have entered the market offering Limited Companies via the Internet at prices lower than the traditional service. But many of these online services are quite complex.

Now the best known and trusted name in the market is offering an Internet based service you can trust, that is easy to use, and at the lowest price.

www.sdgonline.co.uk

Thinking of giving up your day job?

Things to consider before starting your Business:

Starting a business is one of the most serious decisions that a person can take in life. Positively, it often results in higher income levels than one could achieve as an employee together with the unique buzz of being your own boss but conversely it also can be stressful, will demand longer working hours and will probably reduce your ability to take long holidays. Ask yourself and others if you have what it takes to be a business owner. Being able to set goals, having self-discipline, flexibility, and the confidence to take calculated risks, being willing to market yourself and your business, are all essential characteristics of a successful business owner.

The legal format is one of the most important things to be considered when starting your own business. In essence there are three main structures: unincorporated business (sole trader, partnership), a Limited Liability Partnership or Limited Company. In general Sole traders and partnerships can be established with relatively little formality. Both are essentially an extension of the key individuals and whereas the individual(s) has complete control over the business but one should bear in mind that there is no legal distinction between the actual business and the owner. In other words, any liabilities, debts or charges for which the business is liable, the owner is also personally liable. The primary advantage of limited liability entity is that constitutes a separate legal entity from its owners and the liability of the shareholders/subscribers and officers is strictly limited to their direct investment in the company. Limited Liability Partnership offers a halfway house with some advantages of both an unincorporated business and a company. The choice is important because it will determine the way in which the business is conducted, how you and any other owners can take income from the business and also how it can be funded and you should seek expert advice from the outset to conclude which is most appropriate to your individual circumstances. The risks of establishing your own business are considerably reduced by buying a well-known and established franchise. In many cases, the franchisor can often help with finance, computer software and business methodology. The downside is that if you really are aiming for the heavens then becoming a franchisee is unlikely to result in untold riches!

After starting your business you should aim to keep non-essential costs to a minimum. Many new business people overspend on hardware, expensive computers, printing etc. If your business does not require people physically coming to a shop or office do not waste money on office rental or even employing a secretary. In many cases, a serviced or virtual office will create the right impression at a fraction of the cost of having your own office. Before starting your business try living on the bare minimum to see whether you can get by on less money and put the savings toward your future business. Experts recommend saving two years worth of living expenses - the average time for a business to become profitable - before taking on a full-time venture.

Consider how you wish to market your business. Today there is little doubt that everyone in business, small or large, in trade or a professional, needs a website virtually as much as they need a factory or office. Professional looking website will act as your shop window and upgrading your site to accept on-line credit/debit card payments will also save you both time and money. You should also develop a business network of contacts and experts both in your industry and in the community where you will be doing business – make sure your business cards and office stationery reflect the nature of your business.

So, as you can see, starting a business can be exciting but also costly and confusing. Starting-my-business aims to remove all the hassle so you can concentrate on what matters the most – your business. Services for business start-ups, small and growing businesses include: UK, Irish and Offshore incorporations, VAT Registration, Credit Card Acceptance, Free 8 Page Websites, Virtual Offices, Printing, Accountancy & Company Secretarial Services + much more. Visit **www.startingmybusiness.biz** or contact us on **0845 1300 060** for friendly and professional business and legal advice.

Minna Lehtinen
Senior Business Development Manager

Preface

This is a guide for the aspiring entrepreneur starting in business and for those already running a small unincorporated business who are looking towards expansion. It explains what a private limited liability company is and the protection and advantages of trading with limited liability.

Chapter 1 describes corporate structure and its advantages and explains the procedure for incorporation and registration. Chapter 2 deals with formation and Chapter 3 covers capital structure. Directors' powers and responsibilities are dealt with in Chapter 4, and Chapters 5 and 6 deal with organisation and administration. Since some consideration must be given to what happens if things go wrong, Chapter 7 summarises the repercussions of insolvency, when the real protection given by limited liability comes into its own, and the final chapter sets out the procedure for buying a ready-made 'off the shelf' company. The English version of the various forms and documents regulating company life referred to in the text are reproduced in the relevant chapters.

This book is a guide to incorporation of English and Welsh private limited companies but the Companies Acts apply to Scotland with minor adaptations to take into account the requirements of Scottish law. Company legislation in Northern Ireland and Eire has essentially followed the Companies Acts, including changes introduced by EU legislation.

The law stated is at 31 September 2003 and is based on the Companies Acts 1985 and 1989 and the Insolvency Acts 1986 and 2000, but changes are still being implemented. There are new forms and new fees. However, this book is intended as a guide, not a blueprint for survival, and you are advised to check with Companies House or take expert advice before forming your private limited company and making major decisions about its future.

Crichtons –
"fixed cost" company lawyers

Some firms boast of providing "a wide range of services for a broad range of clients". Crichtons doesn't. We aim to be expert in a limited range of areas, delivering certain services to a clearly defined range of clients. Those clients are limited companies, and those who do business through and with limited companies. Some of the areas of our practice are:

- Company Formation
- Company Debt Collection (for companies/against companies)
- Company Liquidation

Most business people avoid using solicitors because of a perception that they will be charged high hourly fees. Our approach is to have a policy of encouraging clients to see us as a useful cost-effective resource. We don't charge hourly fees – we agree a fixed-fee before doing any work. If a fixed fee can't be estimated then its not a matter we can handle – but in most instances we'll be able to help.

The client has the peace of mind of knowing exactly what the matter is going to cost.

We get involved in business start-ups, help when a successful company has problems getting paid, wind up debtor companies, and assist with insolvency issues when they arise.

Our company law staff are highly committed to our clients' business success. Because of the limited range of services offered we really can do this to a very high standard.

Crichtons has invested heavily in the latest technology which we regard as fundamental to our work. At the same time we remember the importance of providing a personal service that meets the needs of each individual client. We like to think that our clients find us friendly but professional.

The majority of our clients come to us by referral through our client base of small and medium accountancy practices. We market specialist services in company law directly to accountants nationwide. We are very proud of our reputation for these specialist services within the accountancy profession. We are now building on this by marketing the firm to business people directly, for example through this publication and others.

Repeat business is critical to our continued success. That depends on getting it right the first time.

Our clients come from all over – they can meet us in Nottingham or London, or we'll go to them anywhere at all if necessary. In many cases face-to-face meetings aren't required as we can use the phone, post and email to do everything you need.

Here's a scenario made up of a composite of some matters we've helped clients with to give you a flavour of what we do. Obviously, names and some details have been changed to protect client confidentiality:

Dick and Judith wanted to set up a business importing generic inkjet refills. Dick had been in the business as an employee for a large company. We firstly checked his employment contract to make sure he hadn't promised not to compete with his employer. We formed a limited company, appointing Dick and Judith as directors. We arranged for a service company to act as Company Secretary. We advised on VAT registration. We helped set up a bank account for the company. When the company had been successfully running for nearly two years we issued a Statutory Demand to collect £17,500 due to the company from a large stationery-products customer who wouldn't pay. Later, we wound up another debtor. In between, we helped the company appoint new directors, change registered offices, collect other debts and advised on varied company issues. Dick and Judith (and their company) always knew how much they were going to have to pay before we did any work. Every time we did something for them we did it to the highest standard possible – that's why they keep coming to us.

We look forward to helping you too – see our full page ad for contact details.

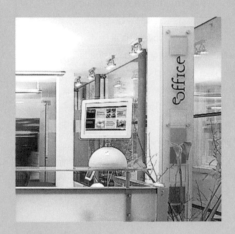

eOffice® offers a fresh approach to working

Established one year ago, eOffice® is an entirely new concept in the serviced office sector. The company provides an aesthetically inspiring, high-tech, professional environment that offers a wide range of 'plug and play' solutions, including hot-desking, high-tech conferencing, virtual offices and dedicated workstations to travelling business executives, SMEs (small or medium enterprises), start ups and other freelance businesses.

Says Pier Paolo Mucelli, founder of eOffice®: "We are creating a new business culture, providing the technology and the surroundings to enable business executives to change the way they work. Our goal is to provide total flexibility and convenience for our customers, making it efficient and easy to do business in a mobile environment. In around one year, we have attracted around 200 companies, looking for flexible and affordable business accommodation with a difference. Several members are start up companies who found that traditional business centres did not provide an environment they wanted to work in and self employed professionals that were feeling the isolation of working from home. These small businesses and individuals appreciate the stimulating workspace at eOffice®, the ability to network with other members and the good value for money of our offering."

eOffice® has recently launched some innovative new services and packages:

- Business Box, offering business address and mail forwarding from £49.99 per month;

- Virtual Office, including business address, dedicated telephone number and live telephone answering from £99.99 per month;

- My first eOffice which offers a flexible office solution from £249.90 per month;

- Hotdesking packages, starting from £2.49 per hour;

- A wide variety of Meeting Rooms from £4.99 per person per hour.

These options are particularly suitable for companies based outside London and require a 'part time' Central London base. No deposit is required and the minimum full time stay is only one month. Members also benefit from links that eOffice® has established with leading lifestyle brands and regular offers for events and shows.

eOffice® has collaborated with leading technology, furniture and interior design specialists, including Herman Miller, Canon, Avaya. Clients can enjoy fast broadband connectivity at each workstation and in each meeting facility. An advanced Wi-Fi network offers additional flexibility, as eOffice® is a 'hot-spot' and now the first serviced office in UK offering totally wireless broadband internet and web-based printing.

The recent installation of PrintMe, in collaboration with EFI, allows eOffice® to offer clients and potential clients a completely wireless mobile print solution. PrintMe stations are connected to all the digital colour and B/W Canon printers distributed around the environment. One of the biggest frustrations facing the mobile business executive is being able to print vital business documents whilst on the move or away from their usual office environment. But with eOffice®'s hot-desking services, clients can now print their urgent documents to any of its four PrintMe-enabled printers, without the hassle of having to connect to the printer with cables or install the specific print driver.

For its flagship Soho centre, eOffice® has selected workstations from the Resolve system of Herman Miller, the leading office furniture manufacturer. These workstations, designed by Ayse Birsel, use 120-degree angles to form open and inviting individual workspaces where people feel comfortable, welcome, and connected. They provide excellent flexibility, informality and privacy for eOffice® customers. The Aeron Chair, designed by Stumpf and Chadwick, enhances the ergonomic aspect of the workstation. The chair adapts to all bodily forms and can be biomorphic or curvilinear, maximising comfort and encouraging healthy seated posture. The eOffice® centre also includes examples of furniture designed by Verner Panton, Arne Jacobsen and Pierre Paulin and from emerging design companies like Kristalia (Udine), byDesign (Birmingham), Antidiva (Milan) and Patricia Adler (London).

MyOffice.net is the recently launched Members' Portal, where the over 300 current members can offer their services, post messages, connect with other members. Social and business networking events are also organized on a monthly basis.

eOffice® is the fastest growing concept in the serviced office sector in London, despite a slowdown in the office market in the past two years. eOffice® represents the most flexible and attractive choice for SME's and individuals wanting a professional presence in the heart of London. The eOffice® solution provides an office instantly on arrival, complete with telephone, fax, broadband internet connection, quiet areas and meeting rooms.

The eOffice® centre is situated at 2 Sheraton Street, London, W1F 8BH.
For further information please call **0870 888 8888**, email **eo@eoffice.net**, and check **www.eoffice.net**

Eventful Management

Many clients approach Wellesley House Business Centre with well laid business plans. In 2000 one such client was Jeff Whiteley.

Jeff had operated for some years as a sub-contractor offering audio-visual services in the business conference and event sector. Whilst he had enjoyed a good level of success, the continued expansion of his business was limited by being a one-man, sole trader, partly because his clients only saw him as a small business.

His business plan was to move up from being the sub-contract technician to being the conference producer. To achieve this the first step was to create that "big business" image, and a business format that could expand as his client base also grew.

Wellesley House Business Centre was able to provide Jeff with a full range of support services starting with forming a new limited company – Conference and Event Management UK Limited. We were also able to advise him about the tax savings and about the running of his limited company.

Until that time Jeff had been working from home, and as a sole trader this restricted the growth of his business because he was not there to answer the telephone all of the time – *not even Jeff can be in two places at once!* "Even holidays were a problem before. I found it impossible to take any time off work."

Wellesley House took over his main business line and we were able to take all his important calls and either take messages or transfer the call to Jeff wherever he was at the time (which could be anywhere in the world). This meant he no longer missed potential opportunities to quote on client jobs and his business began to grow straight away. "Until I used the services of Wellesley House I did not realise how much new business I was loosing through people not being able to contact me or get an immediate response."

Jeff felt that a better, more business-like image for the new company would be created by a "proper" office address. Therefore he used the Wellesley House mailing accommodation address and we were able to receive post and even sign for deliveries, for him to collect whenever convenient.
"My client base now treats me differently because they have the impression of a much larger organisation and they put more trust in my business. And I have the peace of mind that when I am away my business is still being looked after."

In order to keep his business in the 21st century Jeff registered suitable domains including **www.conferenceandevent.com** and set up email and a simple web site using the Wellesley House registration and hosting services. This also enabled us to keep in touch with him even when his work took him around the world to the US, Canada, South Africa or Maidstone!

As Jeff's business grew he employed staff and working from home became impractical. He moved into the serviced offices at Wellesley House where we were able to continue the full support services the growing company needed.

In 2001 Jeff's business entered a new phase and along with business partner Ian Ewan, they incorporated Tech-Link Events International Limited and registered **www.techlinkevents.com**

Both companies use the registered office and company secretarial services of Wellesley House – thus Jeff and Ian can productively use their time on client events and developing client relationships rather than worrying about the management of their companies.

By 2003 the combined turnover of the businesses has grown to almost £900k and their order book is full for the next year.

As Jeff said "We could never have grown our business so quickly and so profitably without the assistance of Wellesley House Business Centre."

*You may contact Jeff Whiteley at Conference and Event Management UK Limited on **01242 571333**.*

1 Why a limited company?

Your business structure is basic to the way you operate: it is the legal framework which determines your share of profits and losses and your responsibilities to business associates, investors, creditors and employees.

Choices

You have three options: operating as a sole trader – running a one-man business – joining up with partners or trading as a limited liability company.

Why a limited company?

Incorporating business activities into a company confers life on the business as a 'separate legal person'. Profits and losses are the company's and it has its own debts and obligations. The business continues despite the resignation, death or bankruptcy of management and shareholders and it offers the ideal vehicle for expansion and the participation of outside investors.

What sort of company?

The overwhelming majority of companies incorporated in this country are private companies limited by shares; that is, private limited liability companies. On 29 June 2003 there were more than 1.7 million companies, including public companies, listed on the Companies Register in England and Wales, with more than 100,500 listed on the Companies Register in

Scotland. In June 2003 between 7 and 8,000 new companies a week were registered in England and Wales and about 100,000 in Scotland.

The vast majority of registered companies are private companies – in March 2000 there were more than 1.3 million private companies, compared with only 12,400 public companies – and the bulk of the companies' legislation, unlike the legislation of most other European Union member states, applies to both public limited companies and small director-controlled family businesses. Private companies, however, cannot offer their shares and debentures to the public but the directors are permitted to retain control by restricting transfer of shares, and some concessions have been made in the requirements for filing smaller companies' accounts and reports.

Limited liability partnerships (LLPs) – the new corporate structure

This is a new form of corporate business structure organised like a partnership, but where the partners, called 'members', have limited liability and the LLP is liable to the full extent of its assets. The members provide the working capital and share profits and the LLP is taxed as a partnership. Disclosure requirements are similar to a company's and the partners have similar duties to directors and the company secretary, including signing and filing annual accounts and putting together the statement of business affairs in insolvency.

Incorporation costs £95 and independent market research commissioned by Companies House indicated that demand for LLP incorporation is likely to come mainly from existing partnerships, including professional partnerships.

Advantages of trading as a limited company

Although LLPs and companies have limited liability, a legal existence separate from management and their members and have their names protected by registration at Companies House, there remain major advantages in incorporating your business activities in a limited company, which can be summarised as follows:

- It has flexible borrowing powers.

A limited company offers some significant benefits to its owners. So whether you already have your own business or are setting one up, you should consider forming a limited company.

What is a Limited Company?

A limited company is a separate legal entity. If you put your business into a limited company you separate it from other assets you own. You will no longer personally own the business. What you will own is the share capital of the limited company that, in turn, owns the business.

The value of your shares will be directly related to the success of the business and, hopefully, will go up in value. As a shareholder all you have at risk is your shares in the company – hence the concept of limited liability.

In contrast, as a sole trader or partnership, in the unfortunate event that something goes seriously wrong with the business, every asset you own – including your house – is at risk.

Taxation

At the lower end of profits generation, limited companies are more "tax friendly" than sole traders and partnerships. For example, a sole trader currently making a profit of £20,000 can expect to pay tax and national insurance totalling £4,480. In a limited company, based on income from dividends and salary, the tax paid might be as little as £1,280 – a saving of £3,200. Whilst the proportionate tax advantage decreases as profits rise, the limited company structure remains advantageous for profits of up to £300,000.

This favourable tax environment also helps with financing assets used in the business, particularly important where you want to use business assets to fund growth.

Is a limited company right for you?

Factors to consider include:

- Trading as a limited company requires separation of personal and company finances. For example, a limited company needs its own bank account

- The personal use by directors and shareholders of company-owned assets could result in tax bills, for example tax on company vehicles

- Finance providers who previously have been provided with personal guarantees will need to consent to the change. Further personal guarantees may be required.

Incorporating your business ...

Before making any decision you must seek professional advice. Discuss with your accountant whether a limited company is right for you and your business. You should note that there are costs involved for forming, and the ongoing administration of, a limited company.

There is a host of details to consider, including:

- Registering your new company at Companies House and with the revenue authorities

- Appointing at least one director and somebody else as company secretary. The company secretary is legally responsible for ensuring that the various statutory information returns are made

- Opening a bank account for the business

- Printing headed notepaper and proper invoices which should carry the full company name, the word "Limited", your registration number, office address and country of incorporation

- Deciding on the financial year end of the company – this can be any date, although most companies choose 31 December or 31 March.

Once established, your limited company must file accounts with Companies House and the Inland Revenue. Other statutory returns must also be made to Companies House. You will risk fines or even prosecution for failing to comply with the regulations.

Chantrey Vellacott DFK's specialists can guide you through all the details of establishing a limited company and ensure that your energies go into growing your business. We can also ensure that, as time passes, you fulfil all your statutory obligations in terms of filing accounts and other information.

For information about how Chantrey Vellacott DFK can help you, contact Mark Lamb on **020 7509 9000** or email him at **mlamb@cvdfk.com**

- The company continues despite the death, resignation or bankruptcy of management and members.
- The interests and obligations of management are defined.
- Appointment, retirement or removal of directors is straightforward.
- New shareholders and investors can be easily assimilated.
- Employees can acquire shares.
- Approved company pension schemes usually provide better benefits than those paid under contracts with the self-employed and those in non-pensionable employment. The level of premium that directors can pay is restricted but there is no limit on the overall contributions paid by the company for the directors, although there is a maximum benefit limit imposed by the Inland Revenue Superannuation Fund Office.
- Taxation: sole traders, partners and partnerships pay income tax. Sole traders' and partners' income is taxed as the proprietors' income, regardless of how much profit is retained as working capital, and interest on loans to the business is taxed as their income. Partners are liable personally and jointly for partnership tax and, if a partner dies, the surviving partners are responsible for partnership tax.
- Directors pay income tax and the company pays corporation tax on company profits, and with current rates of tax company profits earned and retained in the business are assessed to corporation tax at lower rates than if income tax were payable on equivalent profits earned by an unincorporated business.

Limited liability

The main and most important advantage of a private company is the protection given by limited liability. The members' – its shareholders' – only liability is for the amount unpaid on their shares. Since many private companies issue shares as fully paid, if things go wrong your only loss is the value of the shares and any loans made to the company.

You can see the advantage if you compare the position of a sole trader with two separate unincorporated businesses and one becomes insolvent. Without Companies Act protection, the solvent business's assets can be claimed by the creditors of the unsuccessful business. With protection, the creditors usually have no claim.

Protection does not, however, extend to fraud. Company directors have a duty not knowingly to incur debts they have reason to believe the company cannot or will be unlikely to repay. If they do and the creditors lose their money, the directors and anyone else involved in the fraud can be liable and their personal liability is then without limit.

Protection of the company name

The sole trader or partnership can put their names on the door and start trading but there is no property in a name and their only real protection is under the trademarks legislation or by taking legal proceedings in a 'passing-off' action for damages to compensate for loss of goodwill.

The choice of both business and company names is restricted. Company names must be registered with the Registrar of Companies and they are protected by registration on the Registrar's Index of Company Names.

Continuity

A company has a legal existence separate from its shareholders. Once formed it has everlasting life. Directors, management and employees can only act as its agent and it is the company itself which owns property and 'signs' contracts. Shares change hands, management and the workforce may change and the company continues trading, but the sole trader's business dies with him and, in the absence of contrary agreement, a partnership is dissolved on the resignation, bankruptcy or death of a partner. The artificially created company, however, is only killed off by winding up, liquidation, by order of the court or by the Registrar of Companies.

Borrowing

You can increase the company's permanent capital base by a new issue of shares and a company has uniquely flexible borrowing powers.

Ordinary shares can be issued for loans, giving shareholders a right to vote and receive a share of profits by way of dividends.

You can issue preference shares in return for loans and defer repayment to a fixed date, the happening of a specified event or by fixing the rate of dividend. Preference shares do not usually give a right to vote at company meetings and the 'preference' signifies the holder's right to payment of interest or dividend and to preferential repayment of share capital before other classes of shareholders if the company is wound up.

Debentures provide permanent additional capital and can be issued to carry a fixed rate of interest under a fixed or floating charge on some or all of the company's assets. Debenture holders have preference with regard to repayment of capital and payment of interest in a winding up, even if the issue carries no charge on the assets.

Your bank may require to be secured by a floating charge. The charge 'floats' on some or all of the company's assets as they exist or change from time to time and is unique to corporate borrowings. It can cover stock in trade, book debts, furniture, equipment and machinery, as well as goodwill and other unspecified assets; its advantage is that the secured assets can be freely dealt with, mortgaged or sold in the ordinary course of business until the interest or capital is unpaid or there is any other breach of the agreement with the lender. The charge then becomes fixed and the lender can appoint a receiver.

Enterprise Investment Scheme

The scheme applies to new companies only and enables a private outside investor to make a minority investment of between £500 and £150,000 per annum or 30 per cent of the company's share capital and to obtain 20 per cent income tax relief on his stake. Relief on up to half the amount invested in any one year can be carried back to the previous tax year, provided it does not exceed £15,000. The relief is available only during the first three years of the company's business life, or by a self-employed person starting in business or incorporating business activities during the first three years' trading, and usually the investment must be for a minimum of five years. The first disposal of shares is not liable for capital gains tax and there is no restriction on the amount which is deductible in calculating the chargeable gain when the shares are sold. If there is a loss you can choose between income tax or capital gains tax relief. The scheme covers most trading, manufacturing, service, research and development, construction, retail and wholesaling business but there are some exceptions, including financial services, overseas companies and investment and property companies. There is no limit on the amount of share capital that can be issued under the scheme but the details are complicated. If conditions are infringed, tax relief is revoked retrospectively, interest being charged on the relief, which is taxed as a loan from the Treasury; investors should therefore take advice before proceeding.

Outside investment

There are tax incentives for outside investors in small unquoted trading companies under the Enterprise Investment, Venture Capital Trust and Corporate Venturing schemes. Here a 'small' company is one with gross assets of up to £15,000,000 immediately before the issue of the shares purchased by the outside investor and £16,000,000 immediately afterwards.

The Venture Capital Trust Scheme

Companies listed on the Stock Exchange under this scheme invest in small higher-risk unquoted trading companies in the same businesses as the

Enterprise Investment Scheme. The investor obtains income tax relief at 20 per cent of an investment in new ordinary shares with an annual limit of £100,000. The shares must be retained for at least three years, and capital gains tax is deferred on disposal if the gain is invested in shares that qualify for income tax relief.

The Corporate Venturing Scheme

This is another tax incentive scheme to encourage investment in small higher-risk unquoted trading companies. The investor company obtains 20 per cent corporation tax relief on investments in new ordinary shares held for at least three years. Capital gains tax is deferred if the gain is reinvested in another shareholding under the scheme, and relief is also available against income for capital losses net of corporation tax relief on disposals of shares. The investor's maximum stake cannot exceed 30 per cent and individual shareholders in the small company must retain at least 20 per cent of the small company's share capital. Small companies whose income mainly derives from licence fees and royalties are now included in the scheme if their royalties and licence fees arise from any kind of intangible asset that the company has itself created.

Relief for the investor is safeguarded even if the small company goes into liquidation or receivership.

Changes to the schemes

Small companies whose income from royalties and licence fees arise from any kind of intangible asset that the company has created are to be included in the schemes and the investor will be similarly protected if the company goes into liquidation or receivership.

Retaining control

The sole trader and the sole distributor of a single-member private company run their own show, but in a partnership or company the majority rules the business. Protection of minority shareholders under the Companies Acts, however, is hard to enforce and in practical terms is not very effective. Most transactions can be ratified, even retrospectively, by majority vote of the shareholders; if you hold 75 per cent of the voting shares, and act in good faith and in the interests of the company as a whole, the minority share-holders can only question your decisions if they can prove fraud.

You can now form, and change existing companies into, single-member private companies, thus eliminating all possibility of shareholder conflict. As sole shareholder your name and address must be set out in the register of members, together with the date of the change and a statement that the company is a single-member company. The sole member exercises the powers of the general meeting and must minute all decisions. Details of contracts between the sole member and the company must also be minuted. Where decisions are not minuted, the sole member is liable to pay a fine but the decision remains valid.

The 1989 Companies Act provides for the incorporation of partnership companies – companies whose shares are wholly or partly held by their employees – but the legislative framework is not yet in place.

Tax

The sole trader, the partner and the director pay income tax; companies pay corporation tax.

The sole trader and the partners are liable personally to the Revenue for tax on their share of business profits. Under the new Self-Assessment rules, retiring partners take their tax liability with them and when partners die, their tax liability passes to their estates. Partners are separately assessed to income tax on their share of profits. The partnership, however, has to complete a Partnership (Tax) Return setting out the partnership's profits and losses for tax purposes, and showing how they were divided between the partners.

Self-Assessment to tax is based on the current tax year instead of the preceding year's income and you can now 'self-assess' the company's tax bill but you still have to provide accounts drawn up in accordance with the Companies Acts or computations showing how the figures have been arrived at from the figures in the accounts. Tax on profits is paid nine months after the end of the accounting period and shareholders pay tax on dividends as part of their own liability to income tax.

A director's income is taxed at source under PAYE, and interest on loans to the company and share income are included in taxable earnings. There are certain advantages if his or her salary exceeds £8,500 per annum; the first £30,000 on 'golden handshakes' paid ex gratia or as compensation for loss of office is tax free with a reduced rate applied up to £50,000 and redundancy payments can be claimed if the company is wound up.

The company is taxed separately for corporation tax on business profits. Capital gains are taxed at the same rate as income, whether or not they are distributed as income. For 2003/04 the small companies' corporate tax rate is 19 per cent on taxable profits between £50,000 and £300,000. No tax is payable on profits up to £10,000 and there is marginal relief on profits between £10,000 and £50,000. The full rate of 30 per cent is charged on profits exceeding £1,500,000, with marginal relief on profits between £300,000 and £1,500,000.

Capital allowances and various tax incentives for investment in small businesses have made this country a corporate tax haven, so advice should be sought to take maximum advantage of the situation.

There are tax concessions if you incorporate your business and sell it to the company as a going concern in exchange for shares, and a further concession extends to an Enterprise Investment Scheme investor's first disposal of shares in your company.

Companies pay capital transfer tax, individuals pay inheritance tax and both pay income tax on capital gains; for the most part, unless your business is very small, a director is better off than a sole trader or partner taking out the same share of profits.

Want to Form a limited company but never had the know how?

Since the Second World War there have been more inventions emanating from Great Britain than any other country in the world. The entrepreneurial spirit that led to the industrial revolution and development of an immeasurable number of household items has been a part of the national fabric for centuries.

In today's highly competitive market, it's not guaranteed that a new business will survive in its first year, far from it. However, the barriers to entering a market place are surmountable and if you're interested in forming a limited company, it has never been easier!

Many people have a dream, of becoming their own boss, but what is actually involved in the process of forming a company, or making the leap from being a sole trader to a limited company?

A competitive, free market economy means it is a case of survival of the fittest. However, rather than putting people off the idea of forming a new business it should be encouraging for those thinking about doing it to know that as a limited company, personal assets are not at risk, providing of course that you act properly. It is surely a business "no-brainer" for existing sole traders to realise that they can make an easy jump to being a limited company, thereby protecting themselves from personal loss. Further, that there are tax breaks and incentives to reward those with the motivation to do something about their ambition.

The idea that personal assets being protected is useful but the concept of registering Directors, the issue of shares and registering with the VAT man can all be barriers to people who feel this is a concept alien to them. Barriers do exist and not everyone is allowed to form a company.

Who Can Help?
One company that can help you realise your dream without the 'administrative hassle' is CS Company Services. CS Company Services Limited are professional intermediaries to the main high street banks and financial institutions worldwide. Having been established for four years, starting as a

Sole Trader and becoming a limited company in August 2001, they understand exactly the process and advantages of converting and are able to help you through the legal minefield.

What's the next step?
CS Company Service's skill is advising and helping you set up a complete and trade ready limited company, all within 24 hours. All company formations are achieved electronically so no messy paperwork or signatures are required. They are even able to set up your V.A.T. and P.A.Y.E. registration. Each company is formed with Directors, a Company Secretary and Shareholders all registered at company house and with every company registration there is the added extra of a FREE 0800, 0870 or 0871 telephone number.

By using CS Company's services there are several different options available to suit individual requirements. The simplest company package starts at the bargain price of £99, including limited company set up and a business bank account. At the other end of the scale a limited company, registered office, Company Secretary, mail forwarding, full merchant facilities and a choice of four business bank accounts can be arranged for £399.

What if I have a bad credit rating, can I still set up as a Limited company?
Whatever your credit rating CS Company Services prides itself on accepting a wide range of applicants with a varied financial history. Whatever an applicant's circumstances, whether it be county court judgements or have no credit history CS Company Services believe in being able to offer customers from all walks of life access to bank accounts in the UK and abroad, together with company formations. All new companies are guaranteed a business bank account with a choice of banks, HSBC, Lloyds TSB, Barclays or Nat West.

Don't Delay
So, fancy keeping the British tradition of entrepreneur spirit alive? Call CS Company services today and find out if they can help you move up in the world, and be your own boss! All CS need to set you up is the Director's full name and address, including postcode and date of birth. They also require this information for the Company Secretary and require the registered office address.

Call CS Company Services on **0870 4204896**
www.cscompanyservices.co.uk

2

Forming a private limited company

Companies must comply with the rules of corporate organisation and management contained in the Companies Acts. These apply to all companies, large and small, public and private, but some concessions are given to smaller companies and it is simpler and less costly in this country than in any other major commercial centre to incorporate your business activities.

Companies Registration Office

The Companies House main offices in Cardiff and London and regional centres in Edinburgh, Leeds, Manchester, and Birmingham deal with company registrations and the forms and documentation which the company is required to file in accordance with the companies legislation. Notes for guidance on incorporation and for some of the Companies Acts' requirements as well as the statutory forms are available from Companies House free of charge and Companies House offers the directors a CD ROM which sets out details of the requirements of the Companies Act on incorporation. The Registrar's staff are helpful and there is a customer care department which deals with consumer queries, which can be contacted on the following telephone number: 0870 333 3636.

Choosing your company name

Your brand new company's brand new name costs £20 on application for incorporation of your business activities to the Registrar of Companies.

Describing your business activities through your choice of name is effective and cheap advertising but the following restrict your choice:

- The last word of the company name must be 'limited' or 'ltd'. If your registered office is in Wales, the Welsh equivalent 'cyfyngedig' or 'cyf' may be used and company documentation must then also state in English that it is a limited company and the information must be displayed at all places where the company carries on business. Charitable or 'quasi-charitable' companies are exempt from this requirement but a 'quasi-charitable' company must indicate on its documentation that it is a limited company.
- The name must not be the same as or similar to one appearing in the Index of Names kept by the Registrar of Companies.
- Certain 'sensitive' words and expressions listed in Appendix 1 cannot be used without the consent of the Secretary of State or relevant government department. For instance, only authorised banks may use a name which might reasonably be understood to indicate they are in the business of banking.
- The name must not imply a connection with the government or a local authority.
- The name must not be offensive, nor must its use constitute a criminal offence.

Application to register the name is made to the Registrar's Cardiff or Edinburgh office. When permission is granted, the name is reserved pending the passing of a special resolution of 75 per cent of the company's shareholders confirming the name. A copy of the resolution must be sent to the Registrar, together with the registration fee. The name is not effective and may not be used until the Registrar issues the Certificate of Incorporation and permission may be withdrawn before it is issued. The directors are personally liable on contracts made on behalf of the company before issue of the Certificate, so you should allow time for the application for conditional approval to be processed as well as for any delay in sending you the Certificate permitting use of the name.

You can search the index of company names at Companies House or on their Web site, www.companieshouse.gov.uk, free of charge, but it does not show pending applications. If your name is the same as or 'too like' an existing company's, you may be required to change it within 12 months of registration. The time limit is extended to five years if the Secretary of State feels that he has been given misleading information or undertakings or assurances given on registration have not been met; he can direct a change of name at any time if the name is so misleading as to the nature of the company's activities that it is likely to cause harm to the public.

ELECTRONIC FILING: THE SMARTER WAY TO FORM A COMPANY

The background

When electronic filing was first introduced by Companies House in 1998, it was limited to the appointment, termination and change in details of the officers of a company and changes to the registered office address and filing of the annual return. Jordans, as the UK leader in company formations, was asked by Companies House to assist in the introduction of its e-filing service. In 2001, the electronic filing service was extended to company formations and Jordans was one of the first formation agents to be authorised to file electronically. Our service, Incorporator, is a fully electronic web-based service but we also use e-filing behind the scenes as part of our telephone service.

To facilitate e-filing, changes were introduced under the Electronic Communications Act 2000 and the Companies Act 1985 (Electronic Communications) Order 2000. The net effect is that company formations are now faster and easier using electronic means.

The benefits

Enormous benefits are achieved from e-filing. Companies are now formed within a guaranteed 24 hours, although in practice, they are generally formed within a few hours, depending on the volumes going through the system.

Electronic formation dispenses with the need for paperwork. A statutory declaration is not required and neither is a witness to the signature on the Memorandum and Articles. A proposed officer makes an electronic statement that the formation data is in order. When choosing a formation agent, be wary of those who appear to offer a "fully electronic" service. If they rely on issuing paperwork for you to sign, then the service they offer is not e-filing based and incorporation will be slower. Not only does e-filing help to speed up the formation process but it can also be useful if the proposed officers are overseas.

Once the company is formed, Jordans send the certificate of incorporation via e-mail (as a PDF file). We, like most electronic formation service providers, will also supply a paper copy, if required.

With Jordans' Incorporator, if the chosen company name contains a sensitive word such as "group" or "holdings", which can be justified by those forming the company, then the justification can be submitted electronically with the formation to Companies House. Again, this speeds up the process and cuts down on paperwork.

As well as the formation itself, it is now possible to electronically register the following forms relating to company activities:

88(2) Return of allotments (excluding non-cash)

E-filing without using an agent

If you choose not to use an authorised e-filing formation agent but still wish to file documents electronically, you can, but you will first need to register yourself as an Electronic Filing Presenter.

To replace the signature on paper forms and to comply with the Companies Act, all documents received via the Electronic Filing service must be authenticated by (or on behalf of) the company concerned. This is what is known as the Presenter Authentication Code and takes the form of a pre-arranged 6 digit code. This code must be notified to Companies House in writing and recorded by them before any documents can be filed electronically against that company. Every document then filed electronically must bear the relevant company's authentication code or it will be rejected.

Conclusion

Since its introduction in 2001, the growth in e-filing has been rapid. Approximately 60% of all companies formed at Companies House are now registered electronically and 90% of all companies formed by Jordans use e-filing. We have worked closely with Companies House over a number of years and we have a range of software e-filing solutions, which apart from formations also include the e-filing of accounts and annual returns using PCSec, our company secretarial software. Incorporator and PCSec now have a combined total of around 1,000 active company users.

For more information contact:
**Barbara Kelly, UK Corporate Director – Jordans Limited on 020 7400 3317
or e-mail barbara_kelly@jordans.co.uk**

**Mark Bevan, UK Corporate Manager on 020 7400 3316
or e-mail mark_bevan@jordans.co.uk**

The Consumer Credit Act 1974

Registration of the name does not imply acceptance for the purpose of this legislation. If the business requires to be licensed under the Act, you should contact the licensing branch of the Office of Fair Trading, 3rd Floor, Craven House, 40 Uxbridge Road, London W5 2BS, to check whether the name is acceptable to them.

Trade marks

Acceptance of your company name does not mean that it can be used as a trade mark. To ensure that you do not infringe anyone's trade mark rights you should search the appropriate class of goods and services at the Trade Marks Registry or the Trade Mark Enquiries Section, Concept House, Tredegar Park, Cardiff Road, Newport, South Wales NP10 8QQ. The Central Enquiry Unit can be contacted by telephone on 08459 500 505.

Trade mark rights give an automatic right of action against the infringer. Use of an unregistered name may expose you to the risk of a 'passing off' action but compensation is then payable only if the plaintiff can prove that the public has been confused.

The search for a trade mark is technical and you are therefore advised to use a trade mark agent. Details can be found at www.itma.org.uk, www.cipa.org.uk or www.patent.gov.uk.

Trading names

The restrictions on your choice of trading name are set out in Appendix 1 but otherwise almost any name is acceptable provided it is not misleading or, unless you have the consent of the Minister or relevant department, does not imply a connection with the Royal Family, government or local authority, or national or international pre-eminence.

Displaying the company's name

All company documents and stationery must carry the company's full name; its registered number and the address of its registered office must also be included on the company's letterhead. The name must be prominently displayed at the principal place of business and engraved on the company seal (see page 93) and it must not be abbreviated or amended, for instance by changing 'X & Co Ltd' to X and Company Limited'. It must also appear on company cheques, payment then being made 'for and on behalf of the company'. Cheques without the company name are the personal liability of the signatory.

Documents to be completed

The following documents must be completed and sent to the Registrar, so that incorporation and registration can be effected:

- The printed Memorandum of Association, signed by at least two promoters or the promoter of a single member company – the 'subscribers' to the Memorandum – who write opposite their names the number of shares they have agreed to take. They can take up any number of shares and their full names and addresses must be given and their signatures attested by one or more witnesses, giving their full name, address and occupation. Minors, that is persons under the age of 18, should not subscribe as they can repudiate the shares on or before majority. Other companies can subscribe by having a director or secretary sign on their behalf but this should be clearly stated by the signatory signing 'for and on behalf of' the corporate member.
- The printed Articles of Association dated and signed by the subscribers to the Memorandum, their signatures again being witnessed.
- A Statement of First Director(s) and Secretary and Intended Situation of Registered office (Form 10 – see page 26). You must give details of the officers and directors must give their dates of birth, full name and current address. Company officers can, however, apply to the Secretary of State for a Confidentiality Order permitting them not to reveal their usual residential address on company documents, provided they can show that disclosure would expose them to actual or serious risk of violence or intimidation. Details of how to apply are available from The Administrator, Companies House, PO Box 4082 CF14 3WE (Tel: 0845 303 2400). The first director(s) and secretary must sign and date the form of consent to act. The form must also be signed and dated by the subscribers to the Memorandum or by an agent acting on their behalf.
- A Declaration of Compliance with the Requirements on Application for Registration of a Company (Form 12 – see page 29), signed and

dated by the proposed director or secretary named in Form 10, or by a solicitor dealing with the formation of the company. The declaration must be sworn before a Commissioner for Oaths or a solicitor having the power conferred on a Commissioner for Oaths or before a Notary Public or Justice of the Peace, who must also state the place where the declaration was made and date the form.

The completed forms must be sent to the Registrar with the registration fee of £20. A same-day service for incorporation and registration costs £80.

It is at this stage that the proposed name is checked and, subject to approval of the name, the Certificate of Incorporation giving the date of signature and the registered number of the company is issued which must be put on all documents sent to the Registrar.

As from the date of issue of the Certificate, the subscribers form a body corporate – the new company – which exercises its own powers. Prior to that date, however, the company has no existence, so that any business contracts already agreed are the personal responsibility of the signatories.

The Memorandum of Association

The company's constitution is contained in two documents: the Memorandum and Articles of Association. The Memorandum sets out the company's basic constitution and its powers and duties as a legal person. The Companies (Tables A to F) Regulations 1985 (SI 2000 No 3373) as amended available from The Stationery Office give a standard form of Memorandum and Articles; draft forms for both the Memorandum and Articles of Association suitably modified for use by a private limited company can be obtained from law and specialist stationers, which can be further modified for your purposes before you apply for registration.

The Memorandum of Association must state:

- *The company's name*: unless it is registered or re-registered with unlimited liability, the last word of the name, if it is trading for profit, must be 'limited' or 'ltd' or the Welsh equivalent; a Welsh company can file its Memorandum and Articles in Welsh, together with an English translation and you should check with Companies House to see if an English translation is still required.
- *That the registered office is in England, Wales, or Scotland* (London, Cardiff or Edinburgh is also acceptable): this establishes the

The Company

EAC Business Services specialize in Limited Company formations in Great Britain, Republic of Ireland and many offshore jurisdictions such as Gibraltar, Nevis, Bahamas, British Virgin Isles, Belize and Delaware. We offer a fast and professional service at a reasonable fee.

The Services

- The formation of UK Limited Companies within four hours if ordered before one o'clock.

- The formation of Dutch, Bulgarian, Spanish, German and Danish Limited companies – 2-3 days.

- The formation of Republic of Ireland Limited companies within 7 days.

- The formation of Offshore Limited Companies within 3-7 days.

- Full Company Secretarial Services including acting as company Secretary and Nominee Services.

- Business Banking Services in the UK, Ireland, Spain, Bulgaria and many more Offshore Jurisdictions which include an international Debit Card & Cheque book.

- We arrange Business & Asset Finance, Secured or Unsecured.

- Provision of a Registered Office and Business address services.

- Readymade Companies, Same Day Incorporations.

- Limited by Guarantee & Charity Formations.

- Registering a company for VAT & TAX Management.

- Book-keeping and Accounting Services which include Payroll, PAYE, VAT Returns, Year end accounts, Tax Returns and Company Annual Returns.

- We arrange Consumer Credit License and Financial Services.

- Patents, Trademarks and Copyrights in the UK and overseas.

Offshore Services

We provide professional advice for our clients. Companies are incorporated offshore to avoid high tax bills, retention of internationally earned profits, transferring ownership of properties without liability to tax holding fees, and for other purposes such as insurance, banking, trusts etc. Depending on the requirements of a client, we will outline the benefits of using a particular jurisdiction. The main offshore jurisdictions we can provide formations and services in are: Gibraltar, Bahamas, British Virgin Isles, Delaware Isle of Man & Belize. There are many advantages of these offshore areas and we can assist you in making the right choice. We also offer the service of Registered Office facilities, Nominee Directors, Company Secretary, Bank Accounts and full company secretarial services in any of the countries you may wish to operate your company. We have the facility in the United Kingdom to offer a full business address service with your own telephone and fax. From here you can run your own 'office' and anyone dealing with the Company from overseas can be led to believe that your business is truly 'international'.

Since 1998, Eac Business Services (Group) Limited and its family of companies have served thousands of business people, solicitors and accountants. We are committed to the core values of Honesty, Value, Service and Customer Satisfaction.

You can rely on Eac Business Services as your long-term partner in business. Eac Business Services has a commitment to excellence in providing you with the finest Corporations, Limited Liability Companies, Limited Partnership and Trusts. Moreover, at Eac Business Services we care about giving our best to our highly valued customers at an economical price.

What are the advantages of incorporation?

One of the primary advantages of incorporation is the limited liability the corporate entity affords its shareholders. Typically, shareholders and directors are not liable for the debts and obligations of the corporation; thus, creditors will not come knocking at the door of a shareholder or director to pay debts of the corporation. In a partnership or sole proprietorship the owner's personal assets may be used to pay debts of the business. Maintaining the limited liability of a corporation requires that the shareholders and directors follow all the rules of governance, including holding annual meetings and maintaining meeting minutes, which is why we offer corporate advice as part of our complete incorporation package.

Companies House
— for the record —

**Please complete in typescript,
or in bold black capitals.
CHWP000**

Notes on completion appear on final page

10

First directors and secretary and intended situation of registered office

[ ]

Company Name in full

[ ]

Proposed Registered Office

(PO Box numbers only, are not acceptable)

[ ]

Post town [ ]

County / Region [ ] Postcode [ ]

If the memorandum is delivered by an agent for the subscriber(s) of the memorandum mark the box opposite and give the agent's name and address.

Agent's Name [ ]

Address [ ]

Post town [ ]

County / Region [ ] Postcode [ ]

Number of continuation sheets attached [ ]

You do not have to give any contact information in the box opposite but if you do, it will help Companies House to contact you if there is a query on the form. The contact information that you give will be visible to searchers of the public record.

Tel

DX number   DX exchange

Companies House receipt date barcode
This form is been provided free of charge by Companies House

v 08/02

When you have completed and signed the form please send it to the Registrar of Companies at:
Companies House, Crown Way, Cardiff, CF14 3UZ   DX 33050 Cardiff
for companies registered in England and Wales
or
Companies House, 37 Castle Terrace, Edinburgh, EH1 2EB
for companies registered in Scotland   **DX 235 Edinburgh**

Figure 2.1 Statement of first director(s) and secretary and intended situation of registered office

Company Secretary (see notes 1-5)

Company name	

NAME	*Style / Title	*Honours etc	

* Voluntary details

Forename(s)	
Surname	
Previous forename(s)	
Previous surname(s)	

Address

Usual residential address
For a corporation, give the
registered or principal office
address.

Post town	
County / Region	
Postcode	
Country	

I consent to act as secretary of the company named on page 1

Consent signature		**Date**	

Directors (see notes 1-5)

Please list directors in alphabetical order

NAME	*Style / Title	*Honours etc	

Forename(s)	
Surname	
Previous forename(s)	
Previous surname(s)	

Address

Usual residential address
For a corporation, give the
registered or principal office
address.

Post town	
County / Region	
Postcode	
Country	

	Day	Month	Year	
Date of birth				**Nationality**

Business occupation

Other directorships

I consent to act as director of the company named on page 1

Consent signature		**Date**	

Figure 2.1 *continued*

Directors (continued) (see notes 1-5)

NAME	*Style / Title	
* Voluntary details		*Honours etc
	Forename(s)	
	Surname	
	Previous forename(s)	
	Previous surname(s)	
Address		
Usual residential address For a corporation, give the registered or principal office address.		
	Post town	
	County / Region	Postcode
	Country	

		Day	Month	Year		
Date of birth					**Nationality**	
Business occupation						
Other directorships						

I consent to act as director of the company named on page 1

Consent signature	**Date**

This section must be signed by
Either

an agent on behalf of all subscribers	**Signed**	**Date**

Or the subscribers

(*i.e those who signed as members on the memorandum of association).*

	Signed	**Date**
	Signed	**Date**
	Signed	**Date**
	Signed	**Date**
	Signed	**Date**
	Signed	**Date**

Figure 2.1 *continued*

12

Companies House
— *for the record* —

Declaration on application for registration

*Please complete in typescript,
or in bold black capitals.*

CHWP000

Company Name in full

I,

of

† Please delete as appropriate.

do solemnly and sincerely declare that I am a † [Solicitor engaged in the formation of the company][person named as director or secretary of the company in the statement delivered to the Registrar under section 10 of the Companies Act 1985] and that all the requirements of the Companies Act 1985 in respect of the registration of the above company and of matters precedent and incidental to it have been complied with.

And I make this solemn Declaration conscientiously believing the same to be true and by virtue of the Statutory Declarations Act 1835.

Declarant's signature

Declared at

Day   Month   Year

On

❶ Please print name.

before me ❶

Signed   **Date**

† A Commissioner for Oaths or Notary Public or Justice of the Peace or Solicitor

Please give the name, address, telephone number and, if available, a DX number and Exchange of the person Companies House should contact if there is any query.

Tel

DX number   DX exchange

Companies House receipt date barcode

This form has been provided free of charge by Companies House.

Form revised June 1998

When you have completed and signed the form please send it to the Registrar of Companies at:
Companies House, Crown Way, Cardiff, CF14 3UZ   **DX 33050 Cardiff**
for companies registered in England and Wales
or
Companies House, 37 Castle Terrace, Edinburgh, EH1 2EB
for companies registered in Scotland   **DX 235 Edinburgh**

Figure 2.2   A declaration of compliance with the requirements on application for the registration of a company

company's domicile which, unless you can show that management and control are elsewhere, means that the company operates under British law and pays British tax.

The registered office need not be the place at which you carry on business and it is often convenient to use your accountant's or solicitor's address. It is, however, the address to which important and official documents are sent, including service of legal proceedings, so it is important to receive prompt notification of receipt of any documents.

The address must be filed with the Registrar when you start business or within 15 days of incorporation, whichever is the earlier date. It can be changed, provided you stay in England and Wales or in Scotland, but the Registrar must be notified within 15 days of the change.

The registered office address, the place of registration and the company's registered number must be put on all business documentation.

● *The objects for which the company is formed*: this clause sets out the objects for which the company is incorporated and specifies its powers. If the company pursues any other objects or goes beyond the specified powers, it is acting *ultra vires* (beyond the powers of) the company.

Under the 1989 Companies Act a general commercial company's bare statement that the object of the company is to carry on any trade or business whatsoever *and* that the company has power to do all such things as are incidental to the carrying on of its trade or business, is sufficient on the basis that the validity of any act done by the company 'shall not be called into question on the ground of lack of capacity'. However, the legislation has not yet been tested in the courts and it may therefore be advisable to include provisions similar to those required under the earlier law, which require the company's objectives and powers to be set out in full. 'To make a profit' is implied but everything else must be specified.

The *objects clause* is divided into a number of sub-clauses. The first covers the main business activity and should state clearly and fully all the businesses and activities that it is anticipated the company will undertake. The second sub-clause is usually a 'mopping up' clause which covers any other business which in the opinion of the directors may advantageously or conveniently be carried on in conjunction with the company's main business.

If, however, the company has been formed for a specific money-making venture, this is its main object and if it does not produce a profit and you have included nothing else, the company must be

The future is what you make it

As some 62% of businesses fail within the first 5 years of existence. Steve Moore, head of business advisory services at MacIntyre Hudson, looks at the steps you can take to increase your chances of survival.

There is a truism in business that failing to plan is planning to fail. To be serious about wanting your business to grow, you need to get serious about sorting out a plan to deliver success. The following are a few basic but reliable techniques to help you.

Begin with the end in mind

The first step to ensuring your business goes in the direction you want it to, is to establish a clear idea of where you ultimately want it to be, when you feel your creative work is done and it is in its final finished state.

To do this it is helpful to consider the following issues:

- What products and services will you be providing?
- Who will be your target customers?
- What levels of sales and profits will you be generating?
- What sort of team will you need to help you achieve this?
- What image will you have?

The clearer your ideas are at this point, the greater your chances of reaching your final destination. It is not that this vision will remain set in stone until it is achieved, far from it, but by considering these issues you are establishing priorities as to what tasks are important to action and which are not critical to moving you forward.

Wherever possible involve your team in these activities – they are sure to have many different ideas that you can harness, and will be far more committed to working on a plan that they themselves have helped to develop than one that is pressed upon them.

Understand your current position

Before starting on the journey you will need to establish where you stand currently.

Do an analysis of strengths, weaknesses, opportunities and threats (SWOT) to identify those internal and external factors that will affect your ability to move onwards, and then try to establish the same information for your competitors – if you are to outshine them and win business from them you will have to understand them first.

Also work out your own sustainable competitive advantages i.e. where you have the ability to beat your competitors now and for the foreseeable future and then make sure your whole team know how to use this information when talking to potential new customers.

Use action plans

There is no point in pulling together a business plan that analyses where you want to be and where you are now, if you don't also work out how you are going to get there. Involve your team in brainstorming ideas that will help you achieve your goals and then prioritise them to make sure you are starting on the most important first. Develop detailed action plans setting out exactly what you are trying to achieve and step by step details of who will do what by when – these are essential if you are to turn your good ideas into reality.

What you can measure you can manage

In order to make sure you are going in the direction you want, you will need to monitor performance through a few key measures, not all of which will be financial. Assess and measure those activities that are critical to the success of your business. Again, including your team in this project will help them to understand and prioritise the areas of their work that are important.

Start planning for the future today.

wound up. The objects clause can be changed but only to extend or vary the approach to the specified business activities, to restrict or abandon them or to sell out to another company. Alterations must be approved by a special resolution of 75 per cent of the shareholders and can be cancelled by the court on the application of a minority of share and debenture holders within 21 days of the resolution.

It is therefore advisable to include everything you might wish to do, setting out several possibilities and stating that any of them can be the main and independent object of the company, in order that your search for profit can be flexible. The standard form is by including a clause stating that 'every object shall be considered a separate and independent main object and none of the objects specified shall be deemed to be subsidiary or auxiliary to any other'.

Following sub-clauses enable the company and the directors to buy, sell and lease property; to construct buildings, plant and machinery; to borrow and to lend; to acquire patents; to issue shares and debentures; to purchase shares in other companies; to enter into partnership and acquire other businesses; to sell the undertaking of the company; to draw bills of exchange and negotiable instruments; to establish associations and clubs to benefit directors and employees; to distribute property to members and to do all such other things as may be deemed incidental or conducive to the attainment of the main objects.

The directors cannot borrow or invest on behalf of the company unless they are given the power to do so in the *objects clause*, so it should be framed to give the widest possible powers. They can also be authorised to make charitable, political or other contributions, although it is advisable to impose some control on excessive philanthropy and speculation by providing that no director can act without the approval of a majority of the board.

However wide your *objects clause*, some acts and transactions may still be *ultra vires* the company and of senior management. Since entry into the EU, however, transactions with third parties acting in good faith and not specifically aware of a restriction bind the company which can, in some circumstances, turn to the director or senior employee for compensation.

● *That the liability of the member(s) is limited*: this means that if the company is insolvent, the shareholders are liable to creditors for only the amount still owing on their shares; if they are paid for in full, they have no further liability. This applies to all the shareholders, including directors and management, although they may have a separate liability to the company as officers.

If the company continues trading for more than six months with only one shareholder, he has sole liability for company debts incurred during that period if he knows he is the only shareholder.

- *The amount of initial nominal (or authorised) capital and how it is divided into shares*: this clause states the capital, how it is divided into shares and the nominal value of each share, usually £1.

The percentage of the capital subscribed in cash or asset value is called the issued share capital. Any balance remaining unpaid is the uncalled capital and the shareholders' liability is limited to this amount if the company goes into liquidation. References to share capital in the company's letterhead must quote the issued/paid up amount, not the nominal figure.

Class rights, attaching to different classes of shares (see below), may also be set out in the Memorandum but are usually set out in the Articles.

- *The name(s) of the subscriber(s)*: your new company must have at least two subscribers or signatories to the Memorandum in the *association clause* which states that they want to be formed into a company and that they agree to take out at least one share each. If you intend to trade as a single-member company, yours is the only signature required as subscriber to the Memorandum.

The Articles of Association

The Articles deal with your internal organisation, the company's relationship with shareholders and their relationship with each other, the issue of share capital, the appointment and the detailed powers of directors and proceedings at meetings.

The 1985 Regulations contain a set of 118 standard Articles which are designed for large public companies as well as the small private company, so they are usually adopted with modifications. For instance, you may wish more specifically to define and restrict the directors' borrowing powers by requiring that loans over a specified amount must be approved by the majority of the board.

Classes of shares

You may want to divide shareholdings into several classes of shares, with different rights attached to each class. The ordinary shares usually carry voting rights and a share of profits (payable as dividend) but shares can be issued carrying increased voting rights or priority in right to dividend or repayment of original capital if the company is wound up. The Articles can set out how rights can be altered or new rights or classes of shares created and, unless they state otherwise, the changes can then be made by passing an ordinary (majority vote) resolution.

Restrictions on issue of shares

The existing shareholders have a statutory right of pre-emption, that is, the right of first refusal, over most new share issues, so they must first be offered to the existing shareholders *pro rata* (in proportion) to their holding at a specified date. The shareholders must be notified in writing of the offer which must be open for at least 21 days. Your private company's Articles, however, can instead give the directors a discretion on allotment of shares (refer to the standard Articles contained in Table A of the Companies (Tables A to F) Regulations 1985 (see page 22)). If the directors are given authority to allot shares, their authority must be renewed five years from the date of incorporation or from the date of adoption of the Article.

Restriction on share transfers

In order to retain control, directors of private companies usually want to restrict the transfer of shares; this must be done by adding a special provision to the standard Articles, which normally provides that the directors may, at their discretion and without having to give a reason, decline to register any transfer of shares.

Often a right of pre-emption (right of first refusal – see above) is also given to the existing shareholding when a member wishes to sell his shares. The appropriate Article will set out the detailed procedure for the offer and refusal, including time limits and the method of valuation, with recourse to arbitration if a price cannot be agreed. It should be carefully drafted at the outset because, although the Articles can be changed, it may be more difficult to agree the terms at a later stage. The small family company's family directors' domestic problems can have a drastic effect on business decisions and you may also have to consider the interests of outside shareholders.

The basic decision is whether or not the directors should be able to block transfers within and outside the family during a shareholder's lifetime and afterwards, and much depends on the personal circumstances of the promoters.

Purchase by the company of its own shares

Companies can now buy their own shares and assist anyone else to buy them, provided the company's assets are not thereby reduced or, to the extent of the reduction, the finance comes out of distributable profits, that is, profits available for payment of dividends.

Table A includes this provision but the procedure is complicated and there are tax implications, so professional advice should be sought before you take action.

Directors

First directors are named in the statement filed on registration and the Articles usually set out the method of electing subsequent directors, and specify the maximum and minimum number of directors. Table A specifies a minimum of two but a private company may operate with one director, although he may not then be the company secretary.

Anyone can be a director of a private company, provided that he or she is not a bankrupt or disqualified from acting as a director under the Insolvency Act. In Scotland the Registrar will not register a director under sixteen. There is no minimum or maximum age restriction in England and Wales but infant directors must be able to sign the required consent to act and you should take legal advice if you want to appoint someone very young. Some foreign nationals cannot be directors and you should check with the Home Office Immigration and Nationality Department, Lunar House, Wellesley Road, Croydon CR9 2BY (Tel: 020 8686 0688) before appointing a non-British director. The Articles usually disqualify anyone who is of unsound mind or who is absent from board meetings for more than six months without consent. A company can be a director of another company; directors need not hold shares but the Articles can provide that they be required to hold a specific shareholding.

Usually a third of the directors retire and stand for reappointment by rotation each year but the Articles can make provision for life-time directorships.

The Articles covering directors' appointment and removal, however, can be changed by ordinary (majority vote) resolution of the shareholders and the resolution overrides any service agreement made between the director and the company, although the director can claim compensation for loss of office on breach of the agreement. The director's position can be safeguarded by giving him sufficient special voting rights on shares owned to outweigh the votes of other shareholders.

Directors' powers

The majority shareholders run the company but in practice the real power is with the majority of the board of directors, who usually exercise their powers through resolutions passed at board meetings. In larger companies the board deals with general policy; day-to-day decisions are left to the managing director and committees of directors. The smaller company works in the same way but in practice decisions are often made by all the directors on a daily basis.

Table A provides that company business shall be managed by the directors and in addition that the directors may exercise all the powers of the company (contained in the Memorandum) to borrow money, mortgage its property and issue securities. However, you may want to add a provision limiting the total amount of debt which the directors can incur on behalf of the company without the prior consent of shareholders.

Directors' salaries

Directors' remuneration and their expenses must be authorised by an appropriate provision in the Articles. Table A provides for payment of such remuneration as the company may by ordinary resolution determine and payment of travelling, hotel and other expenses properly incurred in connection with attendance at directors' and company meetings. Directors are advised also to agree a full service contract with the company, covering salary, share of profits and/or bonuses and reimbursement of expenses to safeguard their position.

General provisions

Other standard articles cover, for instance, the company's lien on shares for the balance unpaid; making calls on members for moneys payable on shares; forfeiture of shares where calls have not been paid; meetings, notice of meetings and procedure at meetings, including voting procedure; keeping of minutes and appointment and removal of officers; declaration and payment of dividends; winding up; indemnity of directors and use of the company seal (see page 93).

The 1989 Companies Act dispensed with the need for a company seal and the signatures of two directors, or a director and the company secretary, signing for and on behalf of the company has the same effect as if the document had been executed under seal. Your standard Articles will require use of a seal and, at the time of writing, the only evidence of title to a share certificate is a certificate executed under seal. An alternative scheme to

The perfect office solution for those of you who have to run around like a blue a**ed fly.

BusinessBase provides access to our quality serviced office space, meeting rooms, kitchen areas and IT support – all without the cost of leasing an office in its entirety.

Come and go as you please, safe in the knowledge that your calls are being answered in your company name, your mail and faxes are being forwarded on to you and your essential business collateral is in safe storage.

With packages starting from 25 hours per week, you'll also have the opportunity to network with fellow business professionals.

For further information on our products and services and for a full list of over 30 UK locations, freephone 0808 100 1800.

Taking the risk out of office space

Finding the right premises for your company at the right price is fundamental for any business. A serviced office can cost-effectively meet modern demands and change with them, says Jamie Vine, head of product development at MWB BusinessExchange.

Are you worried about how to relocate, expand or even just find a more professional address for your business without over-stretching your finances? The UK's serviced office providers may have the perfect solution, explains Jamie Vine, head of product development at MWB BusinessExchange.

In the past decade serviced office providers have radically changed the way that individuals, SMEs and major corporates have fulfilled their office space needs. Today, the range of services, the flexibility of term, technical capability and total cost savings provided are appreciated by every business from the smallest to the largest.

In today's challenging business environment, where businesses find it difficult to plan more than a few months ahead, the flexibility of size and location of office space can be crucial in staying ahead of competitors. Both established and start-up businesses are finding that taking a more flexible approach to where their business is located provides them with the freedom to visit more clients, service more contracts and sign more deals.

Seamless connection

There comes a time when even the most technically-enabled mobile worker needs the assistance of a company which can help manage the image of, and communications coming into, the business while its' staff are travelling.
One solution is a virtual office, such as BusinessConnect, which provides access to a prestigious business address, together with a range of telephone answering and mail and fax management services. In addition, users also get access to meeting rooms and fully furnished offices on a cost-per-use basis for those special interviews and meetings.

As businesses develop to a point where some sort of fixed base is needed, even if it is only on a part-time basis, then a service such as BusinessBase could be the ideal solution. This innovative new office space solution is designed to substantially reduce occupancy costs for those who only need to use an office part of each week.

Clients will simply unlock their cabinet, take a seat and plug in their laptop to start work. They will be provided with a handset, allocated a DDI and given high-speed internet connectivity. Each will work in a shared facility that will provide excellent networking opportunities, while reducing overheads considerably.

For businesses that need a full-time base the flexibility to right-size and be perfectly located to match business needs is critical. By taking space in a business centre they benefit by not having to make any long-term financial commitments, other than three months' rent, so eliminating the risk element normally associated with new business ventures or relocations.

Businesses also get free reception services and can access secretarial support on a pay-for-use basis, which is much more cost-effective than employing temporary staff and can provide cover for holidays or maternity leave. Such flexible services not only reduce a business's start-up and running costs, they also enable businesses to focus their financial resources on their core operations and transfer financial risk away from their business.

Executives from organisations of all sizes are now more savvy when it comes to making decisions on workspace. "Previous experience in running an expanding company had highlighted the pitfalls of taking a traditional inflexible property lease, such as the ongoing liability for building repairs," comments Keith Simpson, managing director of Optimum.web. "So having had good results using hired meeting rooms at business centres I focused my search in this area.

"I eventually decided to take space at the MWB BusinessExchange centre in London's Fleet Street, as the company offered the best possible combination of advantages for my business. I particularly liked the architecture and feel of the building and judging by the positive comments I receive from visiting clients, it definitely creates an impressive image for my business."

Of course, the real advantage of serviced office space is not just that it is cheaper to occupy than taking a conventional lease, but that its inherent flexibility allows organisations to align their space requirements as their business needs change. So they don't have to pay for offices and meeting rooms that are sitting empty and can focus their resources on what they know best – their core business.

For further information on how MWB BusinessExchange can help your business, freephone **0808 100 1800** or visit **www.mwbex.com**

abolish share certificates so that title can be transferred via computer accounts is not yet in operation.

Duties and fees payable

£20 is payable to the Registrar of Companies when lodging documents on formation and the fee stamp is affixed on the Memorandum of Association. Same-day incorporation costs £80.

Incorporation

The company exists from the date that the Companies Registration Office issues the Certificate of Incorporation, which is numbered, dated and signed. The name can be changed after incorporation for £10 but not the registered number, so if you want to trace a company you should quote the number.

Pre-incorporation contracts

You can contract for the benefit of your not-yet-incorporated company, but the company must be specifically identified in the contract by name or description. On incorporation, the company has the same rights and remedies under the contract as if it had been a party to the contract.

If, however, you are still at the organising stage, you may prefer to contract on your own behalf as promoter of the still-to-be-incorporated company. You are then personally liable until the contract and should therefore contract on the basis that you will cease to be liable once the contract is put before the board or general meeting on incorporation, whether or not the company adopts the transaction. Once it is adopted, the contract is replaced by a draft agreement, which is executed by the company after incorporation.

Transfer of existing business to your company

You can sell your business to the company for shares issued at par (face value). Assets and liabilities are taken over by the company and no capital gains tax is chargeable provided the only payment is the issue of shares.

G

COMPANIES FORM No. 88(3)

**Particulars of a contract
relating to shares allotted
as fully or partly paid up
otherwise than in cash**

88(3)

Pursuant to section 88(3) of the Companies Act 1985

Please do not
write in
this margin

Note: This form is only for use when the contract
has not been reduced to writing

Please complete
legibly, preferably
in block type, or
bold block lettering

To the Registrar of Companies
(Address overleaf)

For official use

Company number

Please do not
write in the space
below. For Inland
Revenue use only

The particulars must be stamped with the same stamp duty as would have been payable if
the contract had been reduced to writing. A reduced rate of ad valorem duty may be
available if this form is properly certified at the appropriate amount.

Name of company

* insert full name
of company

gives the following particulars of a contract which has not been reduced to writing

1 The number of shares allotted as fully or partly paid up otherwise than in cash	
2 The nominal value of each such share	£
3a The amount of such nominal value to be considered as paid up on each share otherwise than in cash	£
b The value of each share allotted i.e. the nominal value and any premium	£
c The amount to be considered as paid up in respect of b	£
4 If the consideration for the allotment of such shares is services, or any consideration other than that mentioned below in 8, state the nature and amount of such consideration, and the number of shares allotted	

Presentor's name address and
reference (if any):

For official Use

Capital Section

Post room

Page 1

Figure 2.3 Particulars of a contract relating to shares allotted as fully or
partly paid up otherwise than in cash

5 If the allotment is a bonus issue, state the amount of reserves capitalised in respect of this issue

£

6 If the allotment is made in consideration of the release of a debt, e.g., a director's loan account, state the amount released

£

7 If the allotment is made in connection with the conversion of loan stock, state the amount of stock converted in respect of this issue

£

8 If the allotment is made in satisfaction or part satisfaction of the purchase price of property, give below:

a brief description of property:

b *full particulars of the manner in which the purchase price is to be satisfied*

£   p

Amount of consideration payable in cash or bills ....

Amount of consideration payable in debentures, etc......

Amount of consideration payable in shares ....

Liabilities of the vendor assumed by the purchaser:

Amounts due on mortgages of freeholds and/or

leaseholds including interest to date of sale ....

Hire purchase etc debts in respect of goods acquired ...

Other liabilities of the vendor,..

Any other consideration ....

Page 2

Figure 2.3 *continued*

9 Give full particulars in the form of the following table, of the property which is the subject of the sale, showing in detail how the total purchase price is apportioned between the respective heads:

£

Legal estates in freehold property and fixed plant and machinery and other fixtures thereon* ....

Legal estates in leasehold property* ....

Fixed plant and machinery on leasehold property (including tenants', trade and other fixtures) ....

Equitable interests in freehold or leasehold property* ....

Loose plant and machinery, stock-in-trade and other chattels (plant and machinery should not be included under this head unless it was in actual state of severance on the date of the sale) ....

Goods, wares and merchandise subject to hire purchase or other agreements (written down value) ....

Goodwill and benefit of contracts ....

Patents, designs, trademarks, licences, copyrights, etc.

Book and other debts ....

Cash in hand and at bank on current account, bills, notes, etc ....

Cash on deposit at bank or elsewhere ....

Shares, debentures and other investments ....

Other property ....

Signed   Designation‡   Date

Certificate of value§

It is certified that the transaction effected by the contract does not form part of a larger transaction or series of transactions in respect of which the amount or value, or aggregate amount or value, of the consideration exceeds £

Signed   Date

Page 3   Signed   Date

Figure 2.3 *continued*

A formal transfer agreement should be executed transferring existing assets and liabilities to the company on incorporation, but professional advice should be sought as to the tax and legal aspects of transfer. It is advisable to provide a proper valuation of the assets transferred, although you are not obliged to do so and you should formally disclose details of the transactions to shareholders even if this is a formality at this early stage when the company may have only one or two shareholders. Full details should be put on file and the sale should be properly minuted when the transaction is adopted at the first general meeting.

The sale agreement or prescribed form of details of the sale and Form 88(3) – see page 43 – must be lodged with the Registrar within one month of the transaction. A stamp duty of 15 per cent *ad valorem* (according to value) is payable on transfer of some assets including goodwill and some debts, but there is no charge to duty if the total consideration does not exceed £60,000 and the agreement contains a Certificate of Value, which certifies that 'the transaction hereby effected does not form part of a larger transaction or a series of transactions in respect of which the amount or value or aggregate amount or value of the consideration exceeds £60,000'.

Duty of 1 per cent applies to transactions up to £250,000 and 3 per cent up to £500,000 and the Certificate must then state that the transaction is within the relevant limit of £250,000 or £500,000. No Certificate of Value is required for transactions of over £500,000 and duty is then payable at 4 per cent. Stamp duty is payable on the purchase of stocks and shares. Duty is £5 per £1,000 increasing to £50 on a purchase price of £10,000, which increases to 0.5 per cent on purchases of over £10,000 rounded up to the next multiple of £5.

What about tax?

A major benefit of incorporation for the self-employed is the zero rate corporation tax band on the first £10,000 of company profits.

In addition to the zero rate of tax, directors paying themselves a small salary set at the personal allowance level of £4,615, and all profit over this amount as dividends, will avoid both flat rate Class 2 and Class 4 National Insurance contributions.

Using an extremely simple example, a self-employed person with profits of £14,615 can now avoid all tax and National Insurance and an individual earning profits of £25,000 will, in the current tax year 2003/04, save £3,523 by incorporation.

These benefits multiply in the case of an existing partnership transferring into a limited company. Each of the partners become company directors and take a shareholding in accordance with the terms of their previous partnership agreement. For example, a 4 partner business producing £120,000 profits per annum is incorporated and each of the 4 new directors take a 25% shareholding. A carefully structured remuneration package similar to that above could potentially save the business over £10,600 per annum in tax and National Insurance in the tax year 2003/04.

The following table summarises the position when comparing an identical business, one operating as a sole trader and the other operating as a company:

Adjusted Profits £	Sole Trader Tax £	Ltd Company Tax £	Saving £
25,000	5,989	2,466	3,523
40,000	10,842	6,640	4,202
75,000	25,192	20,898	4,294
250,000	96,942	89,586	7,356

Another point seldom considered is that for higher rate tax payers the gains could increase further if a percentage of profit is retained in the business. This might be a particularly suitable option for a person nearing retirement age, or if the business has erratic earning levels. The individual can then pay themselves across several tax years at a level which may minimise higher rate taxation, even after they cease working full time.

It is always easy to jump on a bandwagon.

However, it is important to work with your accountant to consider the other factors which will need to be taken into consideration. For example, if you work within the subcontract industry you may fall foul of IR35 legislation which dictates how the remuneration can be drawn from the company. If this applies to you then the tax savings outlined above will be largely wiped out. Another important non-financial consideration is that the company will have to comply with the Companies Acts, and file annual accounts at Companies House which will be open for inspection on the public record. Your accountant will help assist with these administrative and reporting procedures but this will probably incur higher fee levels than services provided to the self-employed.

Several other factors should also be on your list when approaching your accountant to discuss how matters affect you. These include:

- What, if any, will be the impact of taking steps to reduce National Insurance contributions on my entitlement to state benefits.
- Could the incorporation process affect any established lines of credit in place with my suppliers.

As we have shown, extensive savings can be made if the company is correctly structured and the individual is willing to invest the time to get the foundations and procedures established.

In summary you would be well advised to approach a suitable qualified accountancy practice to assist you with this decision, preferably one with extensive experience in dealing with this type of transfer. This is where we can help. The K2 Partnership Ltd is a Chartered Certified accountancy practice who specialise in serving the needs of the corporate client, from fledgling start-ups to the established business. We work alongside leading company formation agents to provide all the information and resources needed to maximise the benefit of your limited company. Please feel free to call on **08702 42 19 86** or email **enquiries@k2-partnership.co.uk** for a free initial discussion of your own situation and requirements.

3

Capital

The limited liability company is structured for expansion; once incorporated, your business easily assimilates additional participants and capital and you can retain control as the majority shareholder.

Corporate capital

The company can build up a complicated capital structure and a whole range of special terms describes capital contributions.

Initial capital contributions

When two directors each contribute £400 to form a company with a nominal or authorised capital of £1,000, each taking 500 shares with a par or nominal value of £1 each, that £800 is the company's paid-up capital for 1,000 shares in the company. The balance of £200 outstanding is the uncalled capital. This can be called on by the company at any time, in accordance with the terms of the Articles, unless it is later decided (by special resolution) to make all or part of it reserve capital which is only called on if the company goes into liquidation.

Nominal capital is the total amount of share capital which the Memorandum authorises the company to issue and any reference to capital on business documents must refer to the issued paid-up capital.

Shares

Your contribution of capital gives you a right to a share of distributed profits but it does not necessarily fix the proportion to which you are entitled.

Payment can be in cash or in kind, including goodwill, know-how or an undertaking to do work or perform services for the company or a third party.

The ordinary shares issued on incorporation give you a claim to income on equal parts of the company's net assets. If you later issue preference shares, their preferential rights must be met before the ordinary share dividend is paid.

Increasing the company's capital

You can increase the company's nominal capital by issuing more shares if this is permitted by the Articles. The issue must be authorised by resolution of the company in general meeting in accordance with the relevant Article. If there is no provision for a new issue, an appropriate Article can be added (by special resolution of three-quarters of the shareholders).

The new capital can be by issue of ordinary, preferred or even deferred shares, paid for on instalment terms; if the Memorandum does not permit this, however, you will have to vote on an appropriate amendment.

Notice of the increase must be sent to the Registrar within 15 days of the passing of the resolution, together with a copy of the Minutes of the Meeting, the authorising resolution and the printed amended Memorandum and/or Article.

Pre-emptive rights

Existing shareholders have pre-emptive rights to new issues in proportion to their shareholding, unless this is excluded in the Articles, payment is not in cash, or the shares carry a fixed dividend, or the directors are authorised to allot the shares.

Directors' authority to allot shares

The directors' authority to allot shares must be contained in the Articles or granted by the shareholders by an ordinary majority resolution in general meeting. It can be conditional or unconditional and lasts for a maximum of five years, renewable for a further five years.

Rights attached to shares, including the right to dividend, depend on the terms of the company's Memorandum and Articles. If you attach the right to vote at general meetings to only one class of shares, the company can be given a wide capital base but management retains control.

Once rights are attached to shares, whether by amendment to the Articles or otherwise, rights can only be varied by the consent of the shareholders affected, however small the group.

Class rights stated to be unalterable in the Memorandum can only be varied with the consent of all the shareholders but, if they will not agree a change, it may be possible to vary them by way of a 'scheme of arrangement' (see page 105).

Details of some share issues carrying special rights which are not stated in the Memorandum or Articles must be filed with the Registrar within one month of allotment. It is therefore advisable to seek specialist advice if you are considering such issues.

Preference shares come in all guises but they all have some preference over other classes of shares in their right to dividend and/or repayment of capital.

Preference dividends are paid at a fixed percentage rate on the price of the share before anything is paid to ordinary shareholders; you can issue several classes of preference shares, ranking one behind the other in their right to dividend. Their dividends are cumulative unless the Memorandum or Articles state that they are not, so that arrears must be paid before the ordinary dividend is paid. If they are stated to be non-cumulative, a dividend passed is a dividend lost for ever. Participating preference or preferred ordinary shareholders receive their share of any surplus distributed profits after the preference and ordinary share dividends have been paid.

If the company goes into liquidation, the accumulated arrears of preference dividends are payable after the creditors are paid off.

Ordinary shareholders are then entitled to the return of capital, in proportion to the nominal value of their shares, unless the Memorandum and Articles give the preference shareholders priority to capital. Surplus assets are usually split between ordinary and participating preference shareholders.

Redeemable preference shares are similar to debentures (see page 54) and advice should be sought before issue.

Share warrants are usually issued only to holders of fully paid-up shares but they can be attached to, for instance, a debenture issue, with the option to convert them into fully paid-up shares at a future date. They usually pay dividends when the coupon attached to the warrant is sent to the company. Unlike share certificates, however, they are negotiable, so if they are lost or stolen the original holder may have no rights against the company. Sometimes voting rights are attached but the Articles may only permit a vote on deposit of the warrant. Companies usually contact holders by newspaper advertisement only, so they often miss meetings and may not receive dividends promptly.

The share premium account

If you are trading profitably and have built up reserves, the true value of shares is increased. If new shares are issued at more than the par (nominal) value of previously issued shares of the same class, the premium must be transferred to a share premium account, which becomes part of the company's capital. This cannot then be distributed without the consent of the court, unless it is used for a bonus or rights issue, or to provide a premium for the redemption of redeemable preference shares or debentures, but it can be used to write off the expenses of another issue.

Reducing the company's capital

A provision in Table A (see page 22) permits you to reduce the company's capital by buying back its shares. The procedure is complicated, there are tax implications and the penalties for non-compliance include imprisonment and/or a fine, so you should take legal and financial advice before taking action.

Company borrowings: mortgages, charges and debentures

Borrowing

A trading company can borrow and give security without a specific provision in its Memorandum and Articles but you should ensure that your company has the widest possible borrowing and investment powers to avoid problems with lenders and shareholders and specifically exclude the provisions of Table A which restrict the borrowing power of both the company and the directors.

Mortgages

A money-lending company can lodge its own shares as security in a transaction entered into by the company in the ordinary course of its business and any company can mortgage partly paid-up shares for the balance remaining unpaid.

Debentures

You can raise additional capital by a debenture issue. The debenture itself is a document given by the company to the debenture holder as evidence of a mortgage or charge on company assets for a loan with interest. The holder is a creditor of the company, but often holds one of a series of debentures with similar rights attached to them or is one of a class of debenture holders whose security is transferable (like shares) or negotiable (like warrants).

Fixed charges and floating charges

If the debenture is secured by specific assets, the charge is fixed. A charge over all the company's assets – which will include stock in trade, goodwill and so on – is a floating charge, as the security changes from time to time. A floating charge, which allows the company freely to deal with business assets, automatically crystallises into a fixed charge if the company is wound up or stops trading, or if it is in default under the terms of the loan and the debenture holder takes steps to enforce the security.

You can create separate fixed and floating charges and the floating charge is always enforceable after a fixed charge, in whatever order they were made, unless it prohibits a loan with prior rights on the security of the fixed assets and the lender under the fixed charge knows of the restriction. Banks usually include this provision in their lending agreements covering the company's overdraft, so that you may have difficulties if you run into a basic liquidity problem, as cheques paid into the account after a company ceases trading may be fraudulent preferences (see page 124).

Registration of charges

All charges, which include mortgages, created by the company must be registered with the Registrar within 21 days of creation. The fee on registration is £10. Your bank's charge on credit balances is not registrable unless it is charged to a third party.

If the company charges property, or the charge is created, outside the UK, the 21-day deadline can be extended by application to the Registrar before the filing deadline. The extension runs from the date when the instrument creating the charge could have been received in the UK in the normal course of business.

The requirement covers charges made as security for debentures, floating charges on the company's assets including a charge on book debts; charges on any interest in land or goods (except, in the case of goods, where the lender is entitled to possession of the goods or of a document of title to them), and charges on intangible moveable property (in Scotland, incorporeal moveable property) such as goodwill, intellectual property, book debts and uncalled share capital or calls made but not paid. Form 395 (see page 56) is used in registering a mortgage or charge and Form 397 (see page 57) for an issue of secured debentures. Unless registered, the charge is void as against the liquidator and any creditor so far as any security on the company's assets is conferred under the charge and the moneys secured are immediately repayable. If the company does not register the charge, the lender or some other interested person can do so.

If incorrect particulars are registered, the charge is void to the extent of the irregularity unless the court orders otherwise but the Registrar will allow a late amendment to the registered particulars. The company and its officers who are in default in registering the instruments are, in addition, liable to a fine of £200 a day until registration is effected and the holder of the unregistered charge is in the position of an unsecured creditor.

A copy of the certificate of registration issued by the Registrar must be endorsed on every debenture or certificate of debenture stock issued by the company unless the charge was created after the issue.

Copies of every instrument creating a charge which requires registration must be kept at the registered office but it is only necessary to provide a copy of one of a series of uniform debentures.

Charges on registered land must also be registered under the Land Registration Act 2002, and fixed charges on unregistered land registered under the Land Charges Act 1972. The 2002 Act comes into force in October 2003 and you should check with the Land Registry as to requirements.

When a registered charge is repaid or satisfied, a 'memorandum of satisfaction' on Form 403b (see page 157) should be filed with the Registrar.

The Consumer Credit Act 1974

Loans for up to £25,000 including the cost of the credit, where the company is a joint debtor with an individual, must comply with the terms of the Consumer Credit Act 1974. A joint and several obligation by the company and an individual is outside the ambit of the Act.

M

CHWP000

Please do not write in this margin

Please complete legibly, preferably in black type, or bold block lettering

* insert full name of Company

COMPANIES FORM No. 395

Particulars of a mortgage or charge

395

A fee of £10 is payable to Companies House in respect of each register entry for a mortgage or charge.

Pursuant to section 395 of the Companies Act 1985

To the Registrar of Companies
(Address overleaf - Note 6)

For official use

Company number

Name of company

*

Date of creation of the charge

Description of the instrument (if any) creating or evidencing the charge (note 2)

Amount secured by the mortgage or charge

Names and addresses of the mortgagees or persons entitled to the charge

Postcode

Presentor's name address and reference (if any) :

For official Use
Mortgage Section

Post room

Time critical reference

Page 1

Figure 3.1 Particulars of a charge

COMPANIES FORM No. 397

Particulars for the registration of a charge to secure a series of debentures

397

Please do not write in this margin

Pursuant to section 397 of the Companies Act 1985

Please complete legibly, preferably in block type, or bold block lettering

To the Registrar of Companies (Address overleaf - Note 6)

For official use

Company number

Name of company

* insert full name of company

Date of the covering deed (if any) (note 2)

Total amount secured by the whole series

Date of present issue

Amount of present issue (if any) of debentures of the series

Dates of resolutions authorising the issue of the series

Names of the trustees (if any) for the debenture holders

General description of the property charged

Continue overleaf as necessary

Presentor's name address and reference (if any):

For official Use
Mortgage Section   Post room

Time critical Reference

Page 1

Figure 3.2 Particulars for the registration of a charge to secure a series of debentures

---

M

COMPANIES FORM No. 398

**Certificate of registration in
Scotland or Northern Ireland
of a charge comprising property
situate there**

398

Please do not
write in
this margin

Pursuant to section 398(4) of the Companies Act 1985

Please complete
legibly, preferably
in block type, or
bold block lettering

* insert full name
of company

To the Registrar of Companies
(Address overleaf)

Company number

Name of company

* _____

I _____
_____

of _____
_____
_____
_____

§ give date and
parties to charge

certify that the charge§ _____
_____
_____

of which a true copy is annexed to this form was presented for registration on _____ 19 _____

† delete as
appropriate

in [Scotland] [Northern Ireland]†

Signed

Date

Presentor's name address and
reference (if any):

For official Use
Mortgage Section

Post room

Figure 3.3 Certificate of registration in Scotland or Northern Ireland of a
charge comprising property situated there

M

CHWP000

Please do not write in this margin

Please complete legibly, preferably in black type, or bold block lettering

* insert full name of Company

COMPANIES FORM No. 400

Particulars of a mortgage or charge subject to which property has been acquired

400

A fee of £10 is payable to Companies House in respect of each register entry for a mortgage or charge.

Pursuant to section 400 of the Companies Act 1985

To the Registrar of Companies
(Address overleaf - Note 4)

For official use

Company number

Name of company

*

Date and description of the instrument (if any) creating or evidencing the mortgage or charge (note 1)

Amount secured by the mortgage or charge _____

Names and addresses of the mortgagees or persons entitled to the mortgage or charge

Short particulars of the property mortgaged or charged

Continue overleaf as necessary

Presentor's name address and reference (if any) :

For official Use (02/00)
Mortgage Section

Post room

Time critical reference

Page 1

Figure 3.4 Particulars of a mortgage or charge subject to which property has been acquired

M

CHWP000

COMPANIES FORM No. 410(Scot)

**Particulars of a charge created
by a company registered in Scotland**

**A fee of £10 is payable to Companies House in
respect of each register entry for a mortgage or
charge**

410

*Please do not
write in
this margin*

Pursuant to section 410 of the Companies Act 1985

*Please complete
legibly, preferably
in black type, or
bold block lettering*

** insert full name
of company*

To the Registrar of Companies
(Address overleaf - Note 6)

For official use

Company number

Name of company

*

Date of creation of the charge (note 1)

Description of the instrument (if any) creating or evidencing the charge (note 1)

Amount secured by the charge

Names and addresses of the persons entitled to the charge

Presentor's name address telephone
number and reference (if any):

For official use
Charges Section

Post room

Page 1

Figure 3.5 Particulars of a charge created by a company registered in
Scotland

G

CHWP000

COMPANIES FORM No. 244

Notice of claim to extension of period allowed for laying and delivering accounts - oversea business or interests

244

Please do not write in this margin

Pursuant to section 244 of the Companies Act 1985 as inserted by section 11 of the Companies Act 1989

Please complete legibly, preferably in black type, or bold block lettering

To the Registrar of Companies
(Address overleaf)

Company number

Name of company

* insert full name of company

*

The directors of this company give notice that the company is carrying on business, or has interests, outside the United Kingdom, the Channel Islands and the Isle of Man and claim an extension of three months to the period allowed under this section for laying and delivering accounts in relation to the financial year of the company [ending][which ended on]+

+ delete as appropriate

Day   Month   Year

‡ Insert Director, Secretary, Administrator, Administrative Receiver or Receiver (Scotland) as appropriate

Signed   Designation‡   Date

Notes

1. A company which carries on business or has interests outside the United Kingdom, the Channel Islands and the Isle of Man may, by giving notice in the prescribed form to the Registrar of Companies under section 244(3) of the Act, claim an extension of three months to the period which otherwise would be allowed for the laying and delivery of accounts under section 244(1).

2. Notice must be given before the expiry of the period which would otherwise be allowed under section 244(1).

3. A separate notice will be required for each period for which the claim is made.

4. The date in the box on the form should be completed in the manner illustrated below.

0 5 0 4 2 0 0 0

Presentor's name address telephone number and reference (if any) :

For official Use
D.E.B.

Post room

Figure 3.6 Notice of claim to extension of period allowed for laying and delivering accounts – oversea business or interests

4 *Directors*

The private limited company must have at least one director, although he/she cannot also be the secretary; your Articles can specify the maximum number of directors.

Who is a director?

Anyone, with whatever title and however appointed, who acts as a director, is regarded as a director.

Who can be a director?

Anyone can be appointed as director unless disqualified by the Articles except for:

- an undischarged bankrupt, unless his or her appointment is approved by the court;
- someone disqualified by court order;
- the company's auditor.

Your Articles usually disqualify anyone who is of unsound mind or who is absent from board meetings for more than six months without consent. A company can be your corporate director, and directors need not hold shares unless this is required by the Articles.

There is no minimum or maximum age limit but:

- a child must be able to sign the consent to act;
- you should take legal advice if the child is very young;

- the Registrar in Scotland will not register a director under 16; and
- some non-British citizens are excluded – so check for clearance with the Home Office Immigration and Nationality Department, Lunar House, Wellesley Road, Croydon CR9 2BY (Tel: 020 8686 0688).

Appointment of directors

The first directors can be appointed:

- by the subscribers to the Memorandum (who must sign the Notice of Appointment filed on incorporation) unless the Articles permit a majority to act;
- by naming them in the Articles, when the appointment takes effect from the date of incorporation;
- by appointment at the first company meeting;
- by appointment under a specific provision in the Articles.

Additional and subsequent appointments are made in accordance with the Articles and you can provide for appointment by shareholders in proportion to their holdings. The usual provision permits appointment by the board to fill vacancies, or to appoint additional directors subject to a specified maximum. The new director must then retire at the Annual General Meeting following appointment, immediately standing for re-election and, unless the Articles provide otherwise, the shareholders must have 28 days' notice of the proposal.

Details of the appointment of directors must be filed on *Form 288a*, signed by the officer confirming his consent to act but the appointment is effective even if the notice is not filed. The resignation or retirement of directors or the secretary and changes in their particulars, however, must be filed with the Registrar on *Forms 288a*, *288b* and *288c* respectively (see pages 65–67).

Retirement and removal

Usually, a third of the directors retire by rotation each year, standing for re-election at the Annual General Meeting unless the Articles otherwise provide. They are technically out of office until re-elected by the shareholders.

Removal is by a majority vote of the shareholders and the shareholders and the director must have 28 days' notice of the proposal.

The board of directors

The directors cannot act alone and must work through the board which usually conducts and controls company business. Formal meetings are, however, often dispensed with and the board can delegate its powers to one or more board members and appoint a managing director.

Part-time directors. Non-executive directors with financial, legal or technical expertise can be appointed.

Alternate directors who speak and act on behalf of board members in their temporary absence can be appointed if you have an appropriate provision in the Articles.

Nominee directors are appointed to represent substantial shareholders. They must not act solely in their principal's interests but, like any other director, in the interests of the company as a whole.

Shadow directors are persons in accordance with whose instructions the directors are accustomed to act and they have the same duties and obligations as any other directors. Your professional advisers, however, are not regarded as shadow directors.

Directors as employees

Directors are company employees; they have no right under the Articles to remuneration, notice or compensation for loss of office but they have the same rights as other employees under the employment legislation provided they receive a salary. They should therefore be employed under a service contract setting out their terms and conditions of employment, including pension arrangements, the level of contributions to be paid for life assurance and details of benefits in kind.

Contracts exceeding five years must be approved by the company in general meeting and must be available for inspection at the company's registered office or principal place of business. If there is no full written contract, a written memorandum or note of the terms of employment must be included and details of the place of inspection must be sent to the Registrar.

Directors' duties

A director is a constitutional monarch bound by the terms of the company's charter set out in the Memorandum and Articles. He or she can exercise all

Companies House
— for the record —

Please complete in typescript, or in bold black capitals.

CHWP000

288a

APPOINTMENT of director or secretary
(NOT for resignation (use Form 288b) or change of particulars (use Form 288c))

Company Number

Company Name in full

	Day	Month	Year			Day	Month	Year
Date of appointment				†Date of Birth				

Appointment form

Notes on completion appear on reverse.

Appointment as director ___ as secretary ___ Please mark the appropriate box. If appointment is as a director and secretary mark both boxes.

NAME *Style / Title ___ *Honours etc ___

Forename(s)

Surname

Previous Forename(s) ___ Previous Surname(s) ___

†† Tick this box if the address shown is a service address for the beneficiary of a Confidentiality Order granted under the provisions of section 723B of the Companies Act 1985

†† Usual residential address

Post town ___ Postcode ___

County / Region ___ Country ___

†Nationality ___ †Business occupation ___

†Other directorships (additional space overleaf)

Consent signature

I consent to act as ** director / secretary of the above named company

Date

* Voluntary details.
† Directors only.
**Delete as appropriate

A director, secretary etc must sign the form below.

Signed Date

(**a director / secretary / administrator / administrative receiver / receiver manager / receiver)

You do not have to give any contact information in the box opposite but if you do, it will help Companies House to contact you if there is a query on the form. The contact information that you give will be visible to searchers of the public record.

Tel

DX number DX exchange

Companies House receipt date barcode

This form has been provided free of charge by Companies House

Form April 2002

When you have completed and signed the form please send it to the Registrar of Companies at:
Companies House, Crown Way, Cardiff, CF14 3UZ DX 33050 Cardiff
for companies registered in England and Wales or
Companies House, 37 Castle Terrace, Edinburgh, EH1 2EB
for companies registered in Scotland DX 235 Edinburgh

Figure 4.1 Appointment of a director or secretary

Companies House
— for the record —

Please complete in typescript, or in bold black capitals.
CHWP000

288b

Terminating appointment as director or secretary
(NOT for appointment (use Form 288a) or change of particulars (use Form 288c))

Company Number

Company Name in full

Date of termination of appointment — Day Month Year

as director ___ as secretary ___

Please mark the appropriate box. If terminating appointment as a director and secretary mark both boxes.

NAME *Style / Title* *Honours etc

Please insert details as previously notified to Companies House.

Forename(s)

Surname

†Date of Birth — Day Month Year | m |

A serving director, secretary etc must sign the form below.

* Voluntary details.
† Directors only.
** Delete as appropriate

Signed **Date**

(** serving director / secretary / administrator / administrative receiver / receiver manager / receiver)

Please give the name, address, telephone number and, if available, a DX number and Exchange of the person Companies House should contact if there is any query.

Tel

DX number   DX exchange   m

Companies House receipt date barcode

This form has been provided free of charge by Companies House.

Form revised 1999

When you have completed and signed the form please send it to the Registrar of Companies at:
Companies House, Crown Way, Cardiff, CF14 3UZ   DX 33050 Cardiff
for companies registered in England and Wales   or
Companies House, 37 Castle Terrace, Edinburgh, EH1 2EB
for companies registered in Scotland   **DX 235 Edinburgh**

Figure 4.2 Resignation of a director or secretary

Companies House
— for the record —

Please complete in typescript,
or in bold black capitals.

CHWP000

288c

**CHANGE OF PARTICULARS for director
or secretary** *(NOT for appointment (use Form
288a) or resignation (use Form 288b))*

Company Number

Company Name in full

**Changes of
particulars
form**

Complete in all cases

Name

Date of change of particulars

Day	Month	Year

*Style / Title

*Honours etc

Forename(s)

Surname

† Date of Birth

Day	Month	Year

Change of name *(enter new name)* Forename(s)

Surname

Change of usual residential address ††

(enter new address)

†† **Tick this box if the
address shown is a
service address for
the beneficiary of a
Confidentiality Order
granted under the
provisions of section
723B of the
Companies Act 1985**

Post town

County / Region   Postcode

Country

Other change
(please specify)

A serving director, secretary etc must sign the form below.

* Voluntary details.
† Directors only.
**Delete as appropriate.

Signed   **Date**

(** director / secretary / administrator / administrative receiver / receiver manager / receiver)

You do not have to give any contact
information in the box opposite but if you
do, it will help Companies House to contact
you if there is a query on the form. The
contact information that you give will be
visible to searchers of the public record..

Tel

DX number   DX exchange

Companies House receipt date barcode

*This form has been provided free of charge
by Companies House*

Form April 2002

When you have completed and signed the form please send it to the
Registrar of Companies at:
Companies House, Crown Way, Cardiff, CF14 3UZ   DX 33050 Cardiff
for companies registered in England and Wales   **or**
Companies House, 37 Castle Terrace, Edinburgh, EH1 2EB
for companies registered in Scotland   **DX 235 Edinburgh**

Figure 4.3   Change of particulars for a director or secretary

the powers permitted by them which are not reserved to be exercised by the shareholders in general meeting. If he/she is the majority shareholder and sole director, his/her rule may be despotic.

He/she must, however, act in accordance with the Companies Acts and the general law and has three primary duties:

- a fiduciary duty to the company to act honestly and in good faith in the best interests of the company as a whole;
- a duty to exercise such a degree of skill and care in carrying out his or her duties as might reasonably be expected from someone of his or her ability and experience;
- a duty to carry out the statutory obligations imposed by the Companies Acts and other legislation.

Fiduciary duty

Directors in position of trust

This is the duty to act honestly, in good faith and in the best interests of the company, which imposes a trustee's responsibility on directors to take proper care of the assets and to ensure payments are properly made and supported by adequate documentation. Directors must not make a personal profit at the company's expense and must disclose to the other directors at board meetings any interest in company transactions. Disclosure should also be made at general meetings and it should be formally minuted.

The directors' personal interests must not conflict with those of the company and they must not use its assets, including knowledge acquired through the company, for personal benefit.

Directors as agents

Because the company is a separate legal person, a director can only act as the company's agent, acting on his principal's (the company's) instructions, express or implied. For instance, a director's signature on a company contract binds the company but if he/she signs contracts in his or her own name, without any reference to the company, he/she can be personally liable under the contract.

Company contracts

Interest in contracts

Directors' personal interests and the interests of persons connected with them (see page 49), direct or indirect, in company contracts must be disclosed. Disclosure must be to the board, and the director cannot thereafter take part in discussing the transaction. If the interested director votes on the contract, the transaction can be set aside by the company. In some circumstances details must also be shown in the audited accounts (see pages 70–71).

Borrowing from the company

Loans to directors, connected persons and employees

Companies can:

- make loans;
- extend guarantees;
- provide security in connection with loans to directors, shadow directors and anyone connected with them to a maximum of £10,000, if made on the same basis as would apply to someone of the same financial standing as the borrower.

Also permitted are:

- Short-term (for two months) quasi-loans of up to £5,000, if repayable within two months. For this purpose, a quasi-loan is an undertaking by the company to reimburse the borrower's creditor.
- Loans of up to £10,000 if made in the ordinary course of business and on the same basis as would apply to someone of the same financial standing as the borrower.
- Loans of up to £20,000 to enable a director to meet properly incurred business expenses; provided the transaction is approved in advance by the shareholders in a general meeting or made on condition that, if not approved at the next Annual General Meeting, the company will be reimbursed within six months of the meeting.
- Unlimited loans if made in the ordinary course of business and available on the same terms to outsiders.

Money-lending companies

Money-lending companies that ordinarily provide such loans to employees can lend directors up to £100,000 to buy, or pay for, improvements to their only or main residence for tax purposes. This is, however, a maximum from which any other cash or credit facilities already extended to them must be deducted.

There is no limit on loans made by money-lending companies and their 'connections' in the ordinary course of business if they might properly have been made on the same terms to an outsider.

Money-lending companies can also make loans or quasi-loans and extend guarantees to directors and their 'connections', provided the company would give similar facilities to outsiders in the ordinary course of business. For this purpose, a quasi-loan is an undertaking by the company to reimburse a creditor of the director or connected person.

Connected persons

Persons 'connected with' a director broadly comprise the director's partner, spouse, child and step-child, a company with which the director is associated and of which he/she controls at least one-fifth of the votes at general meetings, a trustee of any trust under which the director, the family group or the associated companies are beneficiaries, and the partner of a 'connected' person.

Loans to employees

There is no top limit on an advance made to set up a trust to buy shares in the company for employees, including full-time salaried directors, or on the amount employees may borrow to buy company shares. The company can, however, assist anyone in the purchase of its shares, provided that the company's assets are not thereby reduced or, to the extent of the reduction, the finance comes out of distributable profits.

The assistance can be by gift, loan guarantee, security, indemnity or any other financial help which materially reduces the net assets.

The smaller business has some tax concessions here but the statutory provisions are complicated and you should seek expert advice before calling on your company's generosity.

The Consumer Credit Act 1974

Transactions of under £25,000, including the cost of the credit, must comply with the terms of the Consumer Credit Act 1974.

Use of company assets

Private use of company assets is restricted. Non-cash assets valued at £2,000, or at 10 per cent the company's paid-up share capital, cannot be acquired by the company or handed over to directors or connected persons without the prior approval of the shareholders in general meeting. Approval can be retrospective if given within a reasonable period of the transaction. If annual accounts have been prepared in accordance with the Companies Acts, the limit goes up to £100,000 or a maximum of 10 per cent of the company's net assets as stated in the most recent accounts.

Disclosure

Credit facilities, agreements to arrange credit, and the provision of guarantees and security to directors and connected persons must be disclosed in the annual accounts or the directors' report, unless the company's contingent net liability during the period covered by the accounts does not exceed £10,000. Any other transactions or arrangements between the directors and connected persons must also be included in the accounts, unless the net value does not exceed £12,000 or 1 per cent of the net value of the company's assets to a maximum of £10,000.

Fines and penalties

Credit facilities extended in contravention of the legislation and *ultra vires* transactions can be cancelled by the company, which is entitled to reimbursement unless this is impossible, or the company has been indemnified for loss and damage, or an outsider without knowledge of the contravention might suffer loss. If restitution is not possible, the contravenor and any director authorising the transaction are liable to reimburse or indemnify the company and, in addition, to recompense it for any consequential gain or loss unless they can prove they did not know the transaction was unlawful. If the transaction is with a director's connection, the connected director is not liable if he took all reasonable steps to ensure that the company complied with the Companies Acts.

There is no way to save an unlawful transfer of assets by providing an indemnity through a third party.

Share dealings

There is no restriction on directors' share and debenture dealings, as long as the company is kept informed and details entered on the company's Register of Directors' interests.

Skill and care

Directors must exercise the degree of skill and care that may reasonably be expected from someone in their position with their ability and experience. Professionally qualified directors must therefore act with the care and diligence expected from a member of their profession and, unless they are part-time directors, should devote themselves full time to the job.

Non-executive directors are usually not involved in day-to-day management and the only requirement is that they regularly attend board meetings, but they must exercise an independent standard of judgement and if they are properly to fulfil the purpose of their appointment they should be encouraged to participate fully in board decisions.

Delegation

The directors can delegate their duties but they must be satisfied that they are delegating to a suitable person who is competent, reliable and honest. They cannot simply abandon responsibility but must keep themselves informed as to progress.

Statutory duties

The directors' *administrative duties* are contained mainly in the Companies Acts and the Insolvency Act 1986.

Both the company and its officers can be fined for failure to comply with the statutory requirements, and persistent default can lead to disqualification from acting as a director or from being involved in company management for up to 15 years, or imprisonment. Fines, payable on demand, apply to the late filing of accounts. They range from £100 for accounts delivered up to three months late to £1,000 for a delay of over 12 months and are in addition to fines imposed on the directors in the criminal courts. The criminal penalties for failure to deliver the accounts or the annual return and failure to notify a change of directors or company secretary are set out in Appendix 3. Directors of small companies therefore often pass these duties to their accountants or solicitors (who are experienced in company administration) so that they can concentrate on management. This is an appropriate delegation of duty but the directors are still required to supervise and they are ultimately responsible for ensuring that the company complies with legal requirements.

The *statutory books* and the *annual return* are dealt with on pages 59 and 60. Although the company secretary is responsible for maintaining the statutory books, the directors' duty to supervise requires that they ensure the company keeps proper records and files the necessary documentation with the Registrar in compliance with the statutory requirements.

Directors' liability

Limited liability means that the company is responsible for business debts and obligations. Liabilities can, however, be passed to directors and management but only in specific circumstances.

The directors have unlimited powers to bind the company, whatever the restrictions imposed by the Memorandum, the Articles or the shareholders, provided the person with whom they are dealing is acting in good faith. However, the company can repudiate an *ultra vires* transaction entered into by a director, a connected person or the board. The directors or the board may then be liable to the company but a connected person is only liable if he or she knew that the directors were exceeding their powers.

The directors are liable personally for breach of statutory or other duty or where there is fraud but they are only liable for negligence if they are clearly at fault.

Directors may also be liable personally if they, or the company, to their knowledge act outside the powers given by the Memorandum and Articles or if they contract without reference to the company by, for instance, placing orders without stating that they are acting on behalf of the company. They are also liable on cheques and other negotiable instruments which do not carry the company's full registered name.

Directors are liable for 'misfeasance' (wrongdoing): for instance, making secret profits at the company's expense. 'Nonfeasance' (doing nothing), however, may bring no liability unless it comes within the matters to be considered on an application for disqualification; a director can apply to the court for relief in any proceedings for negligence, default, breach of duty or trust and the court will relieve him of liability if satisfied that he acted reasonably and honestly and, in the circumstances, ought fairly to be excused.

Employers' duties

The legal obligations imposed on employers relating to employees and third parties affected by the company's business activities apply to all employers. Because of the protection of limited liability, claims are made against the company; although the directors are responsible for ensuring compliance with the law, liability is only passed to them if there is fraud or, in some circumstances, negligence.

The directors, the company and the shareholders

Minority shareholders have no say in the running of the business and if management is inefficient a shareholder may be able to do nothing. It is only the company itself – that is, the majority shareholders – who can take action, and provided directors act in good faith and in the interests of the company as a whole, the majority shareholders can do anything permitted by the Memorandum and Articles and can ratify almost any transaction, even retrospectively, in general meeting.

A single shareholder can, however, sue the company in his or her own name to protect his/her individual rights, for example to compel the board to accept his/her vote at general meetings or if there is unfair prejudice, fraud or 'gross negligence'. A group of 10 per cent of the shareholders can call in the Department of Trade and Industry to investigate the company and in some circumstances the court can take action against management. The directors may then lose the protection of limited liability and be ordered to compensate the company or the shareholder for loss.

Directors and outsiders

Third party claims on directors are usually made by unpaid creditors when the company goes into insolvent liquidation and the protection of limited liability is lost if there has been fraudulent or wrongful trading. Liability can fall on non-executive shadow and nominee directors, as well as full-time working directors.

Fraudulent trading is trading with intent to defraud creditors and can arise when cheques are paid into the company's bank account after a company stops trading, even if paid in under the genuine and reasonable belief that creditors will be paid in a short time. Floating charges and loans are invalid if made within six months of a winding up, unless the company was solvent when the loan was made; in some circumstances the directors must repay the creditor and may also be liable to prosecution.

Wrongful trading. Penalties here extend to disqualification and imprisonment but only if it is proved that at some time before the liquidation the company was trading although the director knew, or ought to have known, that there was no reasonable prospect that it could avoid insolvent liquidation.

For 12 months after insolvent liquidation the directors and shadow directors cannot act for a company with the same name. The court's consent is required before they act for a company using its former name or trading name or one suggesting a continuing association with it.

Personal guarantees are a problem only when the company cannot pay its debts and a guarantee on the bank overdraft is probably the most usual undertaking required from directors in support of a company. This is often backed up by a charge on a director's home. The bank usually requires the director's spouse to be a joint and several guarantor to give the bank priority to the spouse's claim to the equity in the property. A director is advised to resist a request for a charge on personal assets, particularly on his home, as a charge given for business purposes removes the protection under the general law given to residential owners. Independent legal advice should be sought before any guarantees are given.

Business leases

Landlords often require directors to join in a lease of company premises as surety. If the company cannot pay rent, the landlord can then turn to the directors for payment and they remain liable until the lease expires, even if the lease is assigned or the landlord consents to their release.

Commercial contracts

Finance companies often require directors to guarantee payments made by the company on instalment contracts. The contracts provide that in the event of premature termination, the full balance is immediately due and payable, and the directors are liable to pay the full amount if the company cannot do so.

Insurance

The company can indemnify its officers and auditors against liability for negligence, default, breach of duty and breach of trust. The cover is for both civil and criminal proceedings, provided judgment is given in their favour, they are acquitted or relief is granted by the court. You may want to arrange additional insurance to cover the unindemnifiable risk, with the party at risk paying an appropriate proportion of the premium.

The Articles must, however, include an appropriate provision giving the company the power to purchase the insurance, and details of the insurance must be included in the directors' report.

Disqualification

Directors may be disqualified:

- on conviction for an offence connected with the promotion, formation, management or liquidation of the company;
- in a winding up, if the company continued to trade with intent to defraud creditors;
- if guilty of a fraud in relation to the company;
- for non-compliance with the Companies Acts, but there must have been 'persistent default', that is, at least three offences within five years.

Disqualification can be for up to 15 years and the court has discretion whether or not to make the order. It must, however, disqualify a director whose conduct in relation to the company, alone or together with his conduct as director of another company, makes him, in the court's opinion, unfit to be concerned in the management of a company.

The Register of Disqualification Orders, maintained by the Secretary of State, is open to public inspection: anyone acting while disqualified is jointly and severally liable with the company employing him for debts incurred during the period of disqualification, and liability extends to anyone acting on their instructions.

The Companies House disqualified directors list gives details of disqualification orders for directors in England, Wales and Scotland. It is on microfiche and is updated weekly.

5 *Running the company*

The price of limited liability is a certain amount of publicity – documentation and reports must be sent to the Companies Registry, where some are available for public inspection on payment of a fee. In addition, you must make regular reports to shareholders and accounts must conform with the requirements of the Companies Acts.

Notices, copies of accounts and reports can be filed with Companies House by electronic means, that is, via telephone, fax, e-mail or by posting them on a Web site. Some forms can be downloaded from Companies House Web site in PDF format and completed on-screen, then printed, signed and returned to Companies House. Information for Forms 288a, b and c (appointment, termination of appointment and change of particulars of directors or secretaries) and Form 287 (change of address of the registered office) can be submitted electronically. You must, however, use the software from a package supplier or in-house software tested with, and approved by, Companies House. Information is available from Companies House Direct help desk on 0345 573991. Forms can also be ordered to be sent to you by post.

Accounts, summary financial statements and reports can also be sent electronically to shareholders, debenture-holders and auditors or, provided that you notify the recipients, published on a Web site for at least 21 days before the general meeting before which they are to be laid. Announcement that notices are on a Web site must contain specified details about the meeting and your shareholders can send proxy forms and other notices to you via e-mail.

The registered office

Your company must have a registered office to which formal communications and notices, including notice of legal proceedings, are sent. The address determines the tax district which deals with the company's return and tax affairs, except for PAYE which is usually dealt with by the local collector of taxes where the wages records are kept.

The address need not be the company's main trading address and it is often convenient to use the address of the company's accountant or solicitor.

Displaying the company name

The company name must be fixed to, or painted on, the outside of the registered office in a prominent position, as well as at each of the company's offices, factories and places of business.

Business letters and other documentation

The company name must appear on all business letters, cheques and other negotiable instruments, order forms, invoices and on the company seal. The letterhead must also show the registered number and registered office address but you can choose to list the names either of all directors or none of them – you cannot list a selection of named directors.

If the company is registered for VAT, invoices must in addition show the VAT registration number, the invoice number, date of supply, description of the supply, amount payable excluding VAT, the rate of VAT and the amount, the rate of any cash discount and the customer's name and address.

Directors

The appointment and removal of directors and their obligations are dealt with in Chapter 4 and you may want to appoint a managing director, although he has no specific powers under the Companies Acts. His authority is based entirely on the terms and conditions of his service contract or those imposed by the board.

Table A (see page 22) enables the directors to delegate any of their powers to the managing director, who often looks after day-to-day management although he will not usually exercise the company's borrowing powers.

The chairman is the director who chairs board and general meetings. He can be named in the Articles, be appointed at the first directors' meeting to hold office for a specified period, or be appointed at each meeting to act as chairman. Table A gives him a casting vote if there is deadlock on the board and he has no other special powers although they can be set out in the Articles.

Company secretary

The company must have a company secretary, who can also be a director provided he is not the sole director. The secretary has important duties and obligations; Table A provides that he or she be appointed by the directors for such term at such remuneration and on such conditions as they may think fit and they can also remove him/her.

The secretary is the company's chief administrative officer with ostensible authority in day-to-day administrative matters. His/her duties include the convening of board and company meetings, taking minutes of meetings, keeping the company's statutory books up to date, filing returns and forms with the Registrar and dealing with share transfers and proxies.

The first secretary must be named in the documents lodged prior to registration so his/her appointment should be minuted at the first directors' meeting.

The statutory books

The company secretary is responsible for maintaining the statutory registers and books. The statutory requirements are technical and in many smaller companies they are kept by the auditors, who also file the necessary documentation with the Registrar.

The statutory books are a useful record of the company's business activities and comprise:

The *Register of Members*, which lists the names and addresses of the subscribers to the Memorandum of Association and of all other shareholders, with details of their shareholdings. It must be kept at the registered office or at some other office designated by the directors. Entries can be removed after a person has ceased to hold shares for 20 years.

The *Register of Debenture Holders*, which lists similar information relating to debenture holders.

The *Register of Directors and Secretaries*, setting out the directors, full forenames and surnames and any former names, their usual residential address, nationality, business occupation and details of any other directorships held within the previous five years. The secretary needs to provide only his present and former forenames and surnames and his residential address.

The *Register of Directors' Interests*, listing directors' holdings. This must include details of rights given to subscribe for shares or debentures, specifying the period during which they may be exercised and the consideration in cash or asset value; further information must be entered when the rights are exercised.

The *Register of Charges* with details of mortgages and fixed and floating charges secured on the company's assets, consisting of a short description of the property charged, the amount of the charge and the names of the lenders, except in the case of securities to bearer.

The *Minute Book*. Proceedings at general meetings and directors' meetings must be recorded in minute books; when duly signed by the chairman, they are evidence of the proceedings.

The statutory books can be bound or looseleaf but precautions should be taken against falsification. They must be kept at the registered office or other place of business designated by the directors and available for inspection by shareholders without charge for at least two hours a day and copies must be provided on payment of a fee. Creditors as well as shareholders are entitled to inspect copies of the instruments creating registrable charges and the register without charge and they can also be inspected by outsiders on payment of a fee. Access to minutes of directors' meetings is available only to the directors, the secretary and the auditors and the office may be closed and the books inaccessible for up to 30 days, provided you advertise the closure. A full list of the books, registers and documents which must be available for inspection is set out in Appendix 4.

Annual return

Each year an annual return must be filed with the Registrar on *Form 363a* (see page 83). The return is made up to the 'return date', which is the anniversary of incorporation or, if the last return was made on a different date, on the anniversary of that date. The return basically summarises some of the information in the statutory books and changes during the year, including details of issued shares, a list of past and present shareholders, and details of directors and shadow directors (including their dates of birth) and of the secretary. Appointment of new directors, however, must be filed on *Form 288a* and the resignation or retirement of directors or the secretary and changes in their particulars on *Forms 288b* and *288c* respectively (see pp 65,

66 and 67). A change in the registered office address must be filed on *Form 287*.

The classification scheme giving a company's 'type' is the same as that used for VAT trade classification, with the addition of three extra codes. Copies of VAT trade classifications are available from your local VAT enquiry office free of charge.

A copy of the annual return signed by a director or the secretary must be sent to the Registrar, with the registration fee of £15, within 28 days of the return date (see page 81).

If you have less than 21 shareholders, Companies House will send you its new 'shuttle' Annual Return Form 363s for following years. You must still list all the shareholders, but the company's capital and shareholder information is pre-printed and the form is sent with a covering letter stating when the return must be filed and what information, if any, is required to complete the return.

If an annual return is not filed, the company and the directors are liable to fines (see page 61).

The accounts

Accounting reference date

Your newly incorporated company's accounting reference date – the date to which it will make up accounts each year (ARD) – is the last day of the month in which the anniversary of incorporation falls plus or minus seven days. For instance, your company incorporated on 16 April 2003 would have an ARD of 30 April and its accounts would cover the period from 30 April 2003 to 30 April 2004, plus or minus seven days. Accounts filed with a made-up date other than the ARD will be rejected by the Registrar and the company and directors will be liable to the fines set out on page 161.

The first accounting reference period starts on incorporation. Subsequent periods begin after the end of the previous period and are for 12 months unless the date is changed on application to the Registrar on Form 225 (see page 89) during the accounting year or during the period allowed for delivery of the accounts to the Registrar or to the Secretary of State for Trade and Industry (see page 111).

Accounting records

The Companies Acts require companies to keep accounting records to show and explain company transactions and reflect the company's financial

COMPANIES HOUSE

363a

Please complete in typescript,
or in bold black capitals.

Annual Return

Company Number

Company Name in full

*F 3 6 3 A 0 1 2 *

Date of this return *(See note 1)*
The information in this return is made up to

Day	Month	Year

Date of next return *(See note 2)*
If you wish to make your next return
to a date earlier than the anniversary
of this return please show the date here.
Companies House will then send a form
at the appropriate time.

Day	Month	Year

Registered Office *(See note 3)*
Show here the address at the date of
this return.

Any change of
registered office
must *be notified*
on form 287.

Post town

County / Region

Postcode

Principal business activities
(See note 4)
Show trade classification code number(s)
for the principal activity or activities.

If the code number cannot be determined,
give a brief description of principal activity.

When you have completed and signed the form please send it to the
Registrar of Companies at:
Companies House, Crown Way, Cardiff, CF4 3UZ   DX 33050 Cardiff
for companies registered in England and Wales
or
Companies House, 37 Castle Terrace, Edinburgh, EH1 2EB
for companies registered in Scotland   **DX 235 Edinburgh**

Form revised March 1995

Page 1

Figure 5.1 Annual return

Register of members *(See note 5)*
If the register of members is not kept at the
registered office, state here where it is kept.

Post town

County / Region   Postcode

Register of Debenture holders
(See note 6)
If there is a register of debenture holders
and it is not kept at the registered office,
state here where it is kept.

Post town

County / Region   Postcode

Company type *(See note 7)*

Public limited company

Private company limited by shares

Private company limited by guarantee without
share capital

Private company limited by shares exempt under
section 30

Private company limited by guarantee exempt
under section 30

Private unlimited company with share capital

Private unlimited company without share capital

> Please mark the appropriate box

Company Secretary *(see notes 1-5)*

*(Please photocopy
this area to provide
details of joint
secretaries).*

* *Voluntary details.*

*Usual residential
address* must be
given. In the case of a
corporation, give the
registered or principal
office address.

Details of a new company secretary must be notified on form 288a.

Name   * Style / Title   *Honours etc

Forename(s)

Surname

Previous forename(s)

Previous surname(s)

Address

Post town

County / Region   Postcode

Country

Page 2

Figure 5.1 *continued*

Directors (see notes 1-5)   Details of new directors must be notified on form 288a

Please list directors in alphabetical order.

				Day	Month	Year
Name	* Style / Title					
	* Honours etc		Date of birth			
	Forename(s)					
	Surname					
	Previous forename(s)					
	Previous surname(s)					
	Address					

Usual residential address must be given. In the case of a corporation, give the registered or principal office address.

Post town				
County / Region		Postcode		
Country		**Nationality**		
Business occupation				
Other directorships				

* Voluntary details.

				Day	Month	Year
Name	* Style / Title					
	* Honours etc		Date of birth			
	Forename(s)					
	Surname					
	Previous forename(s)					
	Previous surname(s)					
	Address					

Usual residential address must be given. In the case of a corporation, give the registered or principal office address.

Post town				
County / Region		Postcode		
Country		**Nationality**		
Business occupation				
Other directorships				

Page 3

Figure 5.1 *continued*

Issued share capital (see note 9) Enter details of all the shares in issue at the date of this return.	Class (e.g. Ordinary/Preference)	Number of shares issued	Aggregate Nominal Value (i.e Number of shares issued multiplied by nominal value per share)
Totals			

List of past and present members
(Use attached schedule where appropriate)
A full list is required if one was not included with either of the last two returns.
(see note 10)

There were no changes in the period ☐

	on paper	in another format
A list of changes is enclosed	☐	☐
A full list of members is enclosed	☐	☐

Elective resolutions
(Private companies only)
(See note 11)

If at the date of this return an election is in force to dispense with annual general meetings, *mark this box* ☐

If at the date of this return an election is in force to dispense with laying accounts in general meetings, *mark this box* ☐

Certificate

I certify that the information given in this return is true to the best of my knowledge and belief.

Signed _____ **Date** _____

† Please delete as appropriate.   † a director /secretary

When you have signed the return send it with the fee to the Registrar of Companies. Cheques should be made payable to **Companies House.**

This return includes _____ continuation sheets.
(enter number)

Please give the name, address, telephone number, and if available, a DX number and Exchange, for the person Companies House should contact if there is any query.

	Tel
DX number	DX exchange

Page 4

Figure 5.1 *continued*

COMPANIES HOUSE

Please complete in typescript, or in bold black capitals.

List of past and present members
Schedule to form 363a, 363b

Company Number

Company Name in full

Name and address	Number of shares or amount of stock held by existing members at date of this return.	Particulars of shares or stock transferred since the date of the last return (or in the case of the first return, since the incorporation of the company) by (a) persons who are still members and (b) persons who have ceased to be members.		
	Number or amount currently held	Number or amount Transferred	Date of registration of transfer	Remarks

Figure 5.1 *continued*

position with reasonable accuracy. The directors are responsible for ensuring that the balance sheet and profit-and-loss accounts are set out in the form prescribed in the Acts and that they give a 'true and fair view' of the company's financial position and its transactions.

Records must be maintained on a day-to-day basis to include:

- details of cash receipts and payments on a daily basis, including details of the transactions to which they relate;
- a list of assets and liabilities;
- a statement of stock of goods held at the end of (each) financial year with details of stock takings on which the records are based;
- with the exception of retailers, a sufficient description of goods and services bought and sold to enable sellers and purchasers to be identified.

Records must be retained for at least three years, but if you are registered for VAT they must be retained for a minimum of six years.

The company's accounts

Copies of the company's accounts, comprising the balance sheet, approved by the board and signed on their behalf by a director, the profit and loss account, the auditor's report and the director's report, approved by the board and signed on their behalf by a director or the secretary, must, unless the company has elected to dispense with this requirement (see page 99), be put before the shareholders in general meeting within ten months of the end of the accounting reference period. Twenty-one days before the meeting copies must be sent to all share and debenture holders and to anyone else entitled to be given notice of the meeting, such as the auditors, and copies must be sent to the Registrar. Share and debenture holders are also entitled to receive a free copy of the company's last accounts. There is, however, no requirement to lay the accounts before the shareholders or agree them with the Inland Revenue before they are filed.

The directors are liable to fines for delay in filing the accounts with the Registrar, depending on the length of the delay (see page 161). Companies House sends a reminder before the deadline, which shows the filing deadline date in bold type, and if the accounts are not filed on time a default notice and a demand for payment of the fine is delivered to the company's registered office within 14 days. Appeals against the fine are made first to the Registrar, then to the Complaints Adjudicator and thereafter to the county court.

225

Companies House
— for the record —

Please complete in typescript,
or in bold black capitals
CHWP000

Change of accounting reference date

Company Number

Company Name in Full

NOTES
You may use this form to change the accounting date relating to either the current or the immediately previous accounting period.

a. You **may not** change a period for which the accounts are already overdue.

b. You **may not** extend a period beyond 18 months unless the company is subject to an administration order.

c. You **may not** extend periods more than once in five years unless:

1. the company is subject to an administration order, or

2. you have the specific approval of the Secretary of State, (please enclose a copy), or

3. you are extending the company's accounting reference period to align with that of a parent or subsidiary undertaking established in the European Economic Area, or

4. the form is being submitted by an oversea company.

The accounting reference period ending

| | Day | Month | Year |

is Shortened   † so as to end

| | Day | Month | Year |

Subsequent periods will end on the same day and month in future years.

If extending more than once in five years, please indicate in the box the number of the provision listed in note c. on which you are relying.

Signed   **Date**

† Please delete as appropriate

† a director / secretary / administrator / administrative receiver / receiver and manager / receiver (Scotland) / person authorised on behalf of an oversea company

Please give the name, address, telephone number, and if available, a DX number and Exchange, for the person Companies House should contact if there is any query

Tel

DX number   DX exchange

Companies House receipt date barcode

This form has been provided free of charge by Companies House.

Form revised July 1998

When you have completed and signed the form please send it to the Registrar of Companies at:

Companies House, Crown Way, Cardiff, CF14 3UZ   **DX 33050 Cardiff**
for companies registered in England and Wales
or
Companies House, 37 Castle Terrace, Edinburgh, EH1 2EB
for companies registered in Scotland   **DX 235 Edinburgh**

Figure 5.2   Change of accounting reference date

The accounts must be in English but can be in Welsh if you trade in Wales, when an English translation must be annexed to the accounts sent to the Registrar.

The audit exemption

Small companies with a turnover that does not exceed £1 million and with a balance sheet total of not more than £1.4 million, can file unaudited accounts. Although full accounts can be filed, the requirement is only for an abbreviated balance sheet with explanatory notes. Shareholders are, however, entitled to see the profit and loss account and the directors' report. If delivered late they must be accompanied by an auditor's report.

The balance sheet must include a statement by the directors referring to the relevant sections of the 1985 Act stating that:

- the company was entitled to the exemption;
- shareholders have not deposited a notice requiring an audit;
- the directors acknowledge their responsibility for:
    - ensuring the company keeps accounting records in compliance with the Companies Act 1985; and
    - preparing accounts giving a true and fair view of the company's affairs.
- advantage has been taken of the various exemptions – details must be listed for individual accounts;
- in the directors' opinion the company is entitled to take advantage of the exemption(s).

Shareholders with at least 10 per cent of the company's issued capital or at least 10 per cent of any class of shares are entitled to ask for an audit on giving written notice to the company's registered office at least one month before the end of the financial year.

If turnover exceeds £90,000 but is less than £1 million, the unaudited account must be accompanied by an accountant's report. This must state whether the accounts agree with the company's accounting records, whether they have been drawn up in compliance with the Companies Act 1985 as amended and whether the company is entitled to the exemption from audit.

NB Your Articles should be checked to ensure that you are not precluded from taking advantage of the audit exemptions.

The 'exemption for individual accounts'

The 'small' company, defined as one with a turnover that does not exceed £2.8 million, and/or whose balance sheet total is not more than £1.4 million, and/or which employs fewer than 51 people may file abbreviated accounts with the Registrar. Fulfilment of two out of three of the criteria is sufficient to categorise the company. The abbreviated accounts include a modified balance sheet, although full accounts must still be sent to share and debenture holders. The modified balance sheet must contain a statement by the directors, above their signatures, that they have relied on the exemption for individual accounts on the ground that the company is entitled to the benefit of them as a small company. A special auditors' report must also be filed, stating that in the auditors' opinion the requirements for exemption are satisfied, and their report must reproduce the full text of the auditors' report delivered to shareholders at the Annual General Meeting and annexed to the accounts circulated to shareholders.

The abbreviated accounts are an abbreviated version of the full balance sheet and aggregate amounts can be given for each item except for the figures relating to debtors and creditors. The debtors must be analysed to show separately for each item the amounts falling due after one year. The information required where the directors' total remuneration is at least £60,000 need not be set out, nor need there be a statement (as is required on the full accounts) that they have been prepared in accordance with applicable accounting standards. Accounting policies adopted by the company, details of share capital and debentures, particulars of allotments and the basis of conversion of foreign currency amounts into sterling must be included and, where appropriate, comparative details and figures must be given for the previous financial year.

Contents of the accounts

The accounts of the smaller company must include:

● The aggregate amount of directors' and shadow directors' emoluments (ie salaries, fees, commission payments, expenses, pension contributions and the estimated money value of benefits received in kind). If the total is £60,000 or more, the accounts must instead set out the chairperson's remuneration, amounts received by directors paid more than the chairperson and state the number of directors paid less than £5,000 and how many receive payments between successive multiples of £5,000. Details of total payments waived by directors and payments and benefits received from third parties must also be included.

- Details of loans, credit arrangements and agreements for loans and credit arrangements made by the company with the directors and shadow directors and of any company transactions in which they have a direct or indirect material interest. ('Material' interests are not material if a majority of the directors – other than the interested party – thinks they are not material.)
- Details of transactions with persons connected with directors and shadow directors. A 'connected' person is the partner, spouse, child or step-child of a director or shadow director, a company with which the director or shadow director is associated and of which he controls at least one-fifth of the voting shares, a trustee of a trust under which the director, shadow director or connected person is a beneficiary, and the partner of a connected person. Details of credit transactions, guarantees and securities given for credit arrangements which involve amounts up to £5,000 need not be included but credit facilities extended to company officers (excluding the directors) involving a total liability of £2,500 must be set out.
- Details of directors' share and debenture holdings, and of subscription rights granted to or exercised by, the directors and their immediate family, although these can instead be included in the directors' report.

The *directors' report*, approved by the board and signed by a director or the secretary, need not be filed with the small company's accounts but the directors must report to shareholders. Their report must give a fair review of the development of business during the financial year and of the position at the year end, and state the amount recommended as dividend and the amount, if any, that the directors propose to carry to reserve or retain for investment.

In addition, the report must name the directors and state the company's principal activities and any change in the activities during the year. Significant changes in the fixed assets must be listed, as well as details of directors' interests in shares or debentures at the beginning and end of the year. Details must also be given of any important events affecting the company business and of research and development. Certain details of share transactions, employee training and welfare, and political and charitable contributions must also be specified.

The auditors are required to review the report, so you should ask them for assistance ensuring that everything that materially affects the company's affairs is included.

Disclosing the accounts

The company's accounting records must be kept at the registered office or another office designated by the directors and be open to inspection by the company's officers at all times.

It is an offence to mislead the auditors and they are entitled to access to all the necessary documents and information in the preparation of the accounts.

Auditors

The auditors can be appointed before the first general meeting at which the accounts are to be presented. They stay in office until the end of that meeting unless removed by ordinary (majority) vote of the shareholders. They must be appointed or re-appointed at every Annual General Meeting (AGM) for a term running from the conclusion of the meeting before which the accounts are laid until the end of the next AGM.

If for any reason the company is without an auditor, the directors or the company in general meeting can appoint a temporary replacement. If one is not appointed by the meeting the company must notify the Secretary of State within seven days of the meeting, when the Secretary of State may make the appointment.

The auditors must be members of the Institute of Chartered Accountants in England and Wales, Scotland or Ireland or of the Chartered Association of Certified Accountants. A director or employee cannot be the company's auditor but the auditor can act as the company's accountant, preparing company accounts and VAT and PAYE returns and generally giving secretarial assistance and taxation advice.

Responsibility for the proper administration of company affairs, however, rests with the directors. The auditors' only responsibility is for any loss caused by their own negligence or fraud. Their reports and conclusions must be based on proper investigation and they are entitled to access to all necessary documents and information. If they are not satisfied that your books and accounts properly reflect the company's financial circumstances, this must be stated in their report.

The company seal

The company seal – usually a metal disc with the full name of the company on it in raised letters – used to be required as the company's 'signature' and was impressed on documents that have to be made by deed. These include commercial contracts, leases, share certificates, debentures and mortgages. Two directors or a director and the company secretary also had to sign the document for and on behalf of the company.

Now, the signatures of the two directors or the director and company secretary, signing for and on behalf of the company, has the same effect as if the document had been executed (signed) under seal.

If you want to use a seal, its use must be authorised by the directors and you will have to adopt an appropriate Article to provide that affixing the seal must be evidenced by the signature of a director and the company secretary.

Share issues

The directors must ensure that the Articles are complied with on share issues. The secretary records the issue of shares in the minutes of the meeting at which they are issued, and makes the appropriate entries in the Register of members to show the new shareholders' names and addresses and details of the shares issued.

Entries in the minutes and Register must also be made when shares are transferred.

Share certificates

The secretary completes share certificates which are numbered and state the number and class of shares issued. The certificate is signed by a director and the secretary and, if required by the Articles, sealed with the company seal.

Meetings

The method of calling and running meetings is set out in the Articles but procedure is more closely regulated for full company/shareholders' meetings than for directors' meetings, which can be run in any way that the directors think fit.

Single-member companies

The single-member company must, like any other company, have at least one director and a secretary who cannot also be the sole director. However, notwithstanding anything in the Articles to the contrary, the single member, present in person or by proxy, constitutes a quorum for meetings. A single-member 'shareholders' meeting' must be minuted as such and decisions must be formally notified to the company in writing, unless made by way of a written resolution.

If a contract between the company and a single shareholder who is also a director is not in writing, the terms of the contract must, unless the contract is made in the ordinary course of the company's business, be set out in a memorandum or recorded in the minutes of the next directors' meeting.

The 1989 Companies Act has simplified procedures for private companies and the relevant provisions are set out on page 98. They substantially reduce administration and costs and are particularly useful if there is a major overlap between ownership and management.

The following paragraphs apply, however, if you do not choose to take advantage of the new provisions.

The first board meeting

No notice is prescribed for calling board meetings; provided all the directors are notified they can decide to dispense with meetings, conducting business by telephone or correspondence. Table A includes a provision enabling written resolutions signed by all the directors to be as valid and effective as those passed at a duly convened and held meeting of directors. Otherwise, oral notice is sufficient and if a meeting is called a majority of the directors must attend; if a quorum is required by the Articles, the specified number of directors must be present.

The company exists from the date the Registrar issues the Certificate of Incorporation but a great deal of important company business cannot be dealt with until the first board meeting and it should therefore be held on the same day as, or as soon as possible after, incorporation.

Business will include:

- A report on the incorporation of the company, and the Certificate of Incorporation should be produced.
- Reporting the appointment of the first directors and secretary.
- Appointing the chairperson.
- Appointing any additional directors.
- Reporting on the situation of the registered office and deciding whether it should be changed.

- Adopting the company seal and confirming the authorised users and signatories.
- Agreeing the opening of the bank account and naming the signatories, for instance any two directors or a director and the secretary. Your bank will provide a form of company mandate (agreement) which sets out the necessary wording. This must be sent to them with a copy of the Memorandum and Articles of Association and they will want to see the Certificate of Incorporation.
- The allotment of shares (other than the subscribers' shares) and a record of receipts of any payment received for the subscribers' shares and for any other shares allotted. Sealing of share certificates must be minuted.
- Appointing the auditors and deciding on the accounting reference date.

You may also want to appoint a managing director or chairperson, appoint solicitors, deal with matters relating to the company's trading activities and with general administrative matters, and disclose the directors' interests in contracts.

The meeting must be minuted by the secretary but minutes of directors'/ board meetings are not available for shareholders' inspection; they should therefore be kept in a Minute Book separate from that used for minutes of company (shareholders') meetings.

General meetings

The shareholders acting together in general meeting can do anything *intra vires* (within the powers of) the company as set out in its Memorandum and Articles of Association. In practice, their power to control the company is delegated to the directors and exercised by resolutions passed in general meeting.

The secretary must keep minutes of meetings in the Minute Book kept for that purpose and when signed by the chairperson of the meeting or the next successive meeting, they are evidence of the proceedings.

Voting

The Articles usually provide that voting is by a show of hands; each member, regardless of his shareholding, then has one vote. The Articles also usually provide that the chairperson, or any two members, or a member or members holding not less than one-tenth of the total voting rights, can demand a poll when voting is normally on the basis of one vote per share held. Special voting rights attached to shares are taken into account before deciding whether a motion has been carried on a poll, and usually a proxy (authorised by an absent shareholder to vote on his behalf) can only vote on a poll.

A director's personal interest in a company contract disqualifies him from voting; if he does, the transaction can be set aside.

The Annual General Meeting

This must be held within 18 months of incorporation and once in every subsequent calendar year, 15 months being the longest permitted interval between meetings.

The meeting is more formal than a board meeting and motions must be proposed, seconded and voted on. The main business comprises:

- receiving the accounts and the directors' report;
- proposing the dividend;
- electing directors and re-electing those who retire by rotation;
- appointing or re-electing auditors and fixing their remuneration.

The holders of at least one-twentieth of the voting shares can force the company to present a resolution at the Annual General Meeting and to send their comments about it to all the shareholders. In exceptional circumstances a single director or shareholder can ask the court to order a meeting.

Extraordinary General Meetings

Any other company business is usually 'special' and requires an Extraordinary General Meeting, with notice to shareholders of what is to be discussed. The meeting is usually convened by the secretary, on the directors' instructions, to deal with business that cannot await the next Annual General Meeting.

Subject to the Articles, two or more holders of more than one-tenth of the fully paid-up voting shares can demand that the directors call a meeting within 21 days. In default, a meeting can be called by at least half of those shareholders within three months of the request.

Notice of meetings

Notice of meetings and of what is to be discussed must be given to hareholders and to the auditors in accordance with the provisions of the Articles. They usually specify 21 days for the Annual General Meeting and for meetings called to consider a special resolution, and 14 days for other meetings.

You must give 28 days' notice of a resolution to appoint new auditors or prevent their re-appointment and to remove or replace directors. Notice of the resolution must be given at least 21 days before the meeting, so it is usually convenient to give notice of the meeting and of the resolution at the same time.

Notice is given when posted and assumed to be delivered, but it is safest to include a provision in the Articles that an accidental omission to give notice, or its non-receipt, will not invalidate proceedings at meetings. Usually, you do not have to give notice to shareholders living abroad.

Notice can be waived with the consent of 95 per cent of the holders of voting shares and they can agree not to meet at all, but all shareholders with voting rights must agree before you can dispense with notice of the Annual General Meeting.

Resolutions

Resolutions may be ordinary, special or extraordinary.

Ordinary resolutions are passed by a straight majority of those actually present at the meeting. *Special and extraordinary resolutions* need a three-quarters majority and special resolutions must include proxy votes.

Most company business, including the removal of directors and a voluntary winding up in the circumstances specified in the Articles, requires only an ordinary resolution. Special resolutions are necessary to change the Articles and the company's name or objects and reduce its capital. Extraordinary resolutions are only needed for a voluntary winding up when the company is insolvent and for reconstructions and mergers.

Copies of special and extraordinary resolutions must be sent to the

Registrar within 15 days of the meeting; draft forms of resolutions are set out in Appendix 5.

Deregulation of private companies – the simplified procedures

You do not have to serve notice of resolutions and call and hold meetings, provided the action to be taken can be approved by the company, or any class of its shareholders, in general meeting and provided the resolution is signed by all shareholders entitled to vote at the meeting.

The provisions cover special, extraordinary and elective (see below) resolutions which take effect notwithstanding any provision in the Articles. The proposed written resolution must be sent to the auditors and is only valid if they endorse their statement to the effect that it does not affect them as auditors, or that it does affect them but in their opinion need not be discussed in a general or class meeting, or they make no statement within seven days of receiving it.

The resolution must be minuted as if passed in a meeting and, when signed by a director or the secretary, is evidence that it has been passed in accordance with the Act. It must be filed with the Registrar if this is required for such a resolution passed in a general or class meeting.

However, there are some exceptions to, and adaptations of, the procedure. For instance, written resolutions cannot be used to remove directors or auditors before the end of their term of office, and there are special procedural requirements for:

- written resolutions for the disapplication of pre-emption rights;
- the provision of financial assistance to enable the company to buy its own shares;
- approval of payments out of capital;
- directors' service contracts and their business expenses.

Elective resolutions

With the shareholders' unanimous agreement at a properly convened general meeting, or their unanimous written consent, the company can elect to:

- have no Annual General Meeting;

- dispense with the requirement to lay accounts before shareholders;
- vote annually to appoint auditors;
- give directors an indefinite authority (ie beyond the five-year limit) to allot shares;
- reduce the majority required for consent to short notice of meeting to 90 per cent.

6

Changes after incorporation

Changes made after incorporation involve formalities, and some decisions can only be made by the shareholders in general meeting and necessitate filing forms and copy documents with the Registrar.

The directors are responsible for keeping the Registrar informed and there are penalties if some of the documentation is not filed.

Some of the documentation must be signed by a director and/or the company secretary and some by the chairperson of the relevant meeting. The documents you are most likely to use are discussed in this chapter and listed in Appendix 3 and draft forms of resolutions are set out in Appendix 5.

You can now file notices, copies of accounts and reports with Companies House electronically, that is, via telephone, fax, e-mail or by posting them on a Web site.

You can also send the accounts, summary financial statements and reports electronically to shareholders, debenture-holders and auditors or, provided you notify the recipients, publish them on your Web site for at least 21 days before the general meeting before which they are to be laid. Notification that notices are on a Web site must contain specified details about the meeting and the shareholders can send proxy forms and other notices to you via e-mail.

Change of directors and secretary

Directors are elected, re-elected and removed by a majority vote on an ordinary resolution put before the shareholders in general meeting but the shareholders do not vote on the appointment or removal of the company secretary.

Two directors can be appointed in one resolution, and notice of a resolution to prevent re-appointment or to remove or replace serving directors must be sent to shareholders at least 28 days before the meeting. Notice must also be given to the person concerned and to the auditors.

A director can put his objections to removal to the shareholders' meeting or require the company to circulate his/her written representations. The notice of the resolution sent to shareholders should then state that he has made written representations.

Changes of directors and secretary must be filed with the Registrar on *Form 288b* (see page 66), which incorporates a form of consent to act which must be signed by the new officer. Changes in their particulars must be filed on *Form 288c* (see page 67). It is the directors' responsibility to ensure that the Registrar is notified of a change of directors or company secretary.

Changing the auditors

An auditor is appointed at each Annual General Meeting to hold office from the conclusion of the meeting until the conclusion of the next Annual General Meeting. He must be a member of the Institute of Chartered Accountants in England and Wales, Scotland or Ireland, or a member of the Association of Certified and Corporate Accountants (see page 72). Remuneration, including expenses, is fixed by the shareholders in general meeting.

Appointment is by ordinary resolution of the shareholders and can be made at any time before the expiry of the term of office agreed separately with the directors, so that the auditor may be entitled to compensation for premature termination of the separate agreement.

A retiring auditor or one removed before the expiration of his or her term of office may address the meeting called to appoint a successor, or require the company to circulate comments to shareholders, and the resolution for the replacement should state that the retiring auditor has made written representations. He or she is also entitled to attend company meetings which discuss matters dealt with during his or her term of office.

The directors or the company in general meeting can fill casual vacancies but the appointment must be confirmed by resolution at the Annual General Meeting. Unless the court orders otherwise, a copy of the auditor's statement must be sent to the Registrar.

Special notice of 28 days is required for resolutions appointing new auditors, and to reappoint an auditor appointed to fill a casual vacancy or to remove one before expiry of his term of office.

Notice of removal of the auditors must be sent to the Registrar on *Form 391* (see page 103) within 14 days of the meeting.

The auditor is entitled to attend all meetings of the company and to receive all notes of, and other communications relating to, meetings which are sent to shareholders.

Change of registered office

Changes must be notified to the Registrar, within 14 days of the change, on *Form 287* (see page 104).

Change in the place where statutory books and other 'public' documents are kept

Notices of any change in the place where the Register of Members (*Form 353* – see page 106), copies of directors' service contracts (*Form 318* – see page 107) and their interests in shares (*Form 325* – see page 108) are kept must be filed with the Registrar within 14 days of the change. No time limit is specified for filing a notice of a change in the place where the Register of Debenture Holders (*Form 190* – see page 110) is kept.

Change of name

The company's name is changed by majority vote of the shareholders on a special resolution. A copy of the signed resolution must be sent to the Registrar within 15 days of the meeting with the £10 fee for entry on the Index or £80 for a same-day change. The restrictions on your choice are set out in Appendix 1 and the change is effective from the date of the issue by the Registrar of an altered Certificate of Incorporation.

Increases in capital and allotment of shares

The company's authorised capital can be increased by ordinary resolution authorising the increase. A copy of the signed resolution and *Form 123* (see

10

Please complete in typescript, or in bold black capitals.
CHWP000

First directors and secretary and intended situation of registered office

Notes on completion appear on final page

Company Name in full

Proposed Registered Office

(PO Box numbers only, are not acceptable)

Post town

County / Region

Postcode

If the memorandum is delivered by an agent for the subscriber(s) of the memorandum mark the box opposite and give the agent's name and address.

Agent's Name

Address

Post town

County / Region

Postcode

Number of continuation sheets attached

You do not have to give any contact information in the box opposite but if you do, it will help Companies House to contact you if there is a query on the form. The contact information that you give will be visible to searchers of the public record.

Tel

DX number   DX exchange

Companies House receipt date barcode
This form is been provided free of charge by Companies House

v 08/02

When you have completed and signed the form please send it to the Registrar of Companies at:
Companies House, Crown Way, Cardiff, CF14 3UZ   DX 33050 Cardiff
for companies registered in England and Wales
or
Companies House, 37 Castle Terrace, Edinburgh, EH1 2EB
for companies registered in Scotland   **DX 235 Edinburgh**

Figure 6.1   Notice of passing of resolution removing an auditor

287

Companies House
— *for the record* —

Change in situation or address of Registered Office

Please complete in typescript,
or in bold black capitals.
CHWP000

Company Number

Company Name in full

New situation of registered office

NOTE:

The change in the
situation of the
registered office does
not take effect until the
Registrar has registered
this notice.

For 14 days beginning
with the date that a
change of registered
office is registered, a
person may validly serve
any document on the
company at its previous
registered office.

PO Box numbers only
are not acceptable.

Address

Post town

County / Region   **Postcode**

Signed   **Date**

† Please delete as appropriate.   † a director / secretary / administrator / administrative receiver / liquidator / receiver manager / receiver

Please give the name, address,
telephone number and, if available,
a DX number and Exchange of
the person Companies House should
contact if there is any query.

Tel

DX number   DX exchange

Companies House receipt date barcode

This form has been provided free of charge
by Companies House.

Form revised June 1998

When you have completed and signed the form please send it to the
Registrar of Companies at:
Companies House, Crown Way, Cardiff, CF14 3UZ   DX 33050 Cardiff
for companies registered in England and Wales
or
Companies House, 37 Castle Terrace, Edinburgh, EH1 2EB
for companies registered in Scotland   **DX 235 Edinburgh**

Figure 6.2   Change in situation or address of Registered Office

page 112) must be sent to the Registrar within 15 days of the resolution and no capital duty is payable.

Within a month of the allotment of shares a Return of Allotments form, signed by a director or the secretary, must be filed with the Registrar. If the shares are issued for cash, the form to be completed is *88(2)* – see page 113; otherwise *Form 88(3)* – see page 43 – must be filed together with a copy of the contract of sale or details specified on the form.

If the new issue varies the rights of existing shareholders it should be done through a *scheme of arrangement*, whether their rights are contained in the Memorandum or the Articles. The procedure involves an application to the court so you should take expert advice before taking action; dissenting shareholders can put their objections to the variation both to the court and at the shareholders' meeting.

The directors' authority to allot shares

The directors' authority to allot shares expires five years from the date of incorporation or not more than five years after the date of adoption of an Article giving them the authority. Giving them authority, or varying, revoking or renewing it, requires the written consent of three-quarters of the shareholders or their consent given on an extraordinary resolution in general meeting.

The resolution must state or restate the amount of shares which may be allotted under the authority, or the amount remaining to be allotted under it, and must specify the date on which an authority or amended authority will expire. A copy of the signed resolution must be sent to the Registrar within 15 days of the passing of the resolution.

Changes in the Memorandum of Association

Alteration of the *objects clause* requires the approval of 75 per cent of the shareholders to a special resolution.

Application to cancel the alteration can be made to the court within 21 days of the resolution by the holders of 15 per cent of the shares. If there is no objection the alteration is valid and a printed copy of the amended Memorandum, together with a copy of the signed resolution authorising the change, must be sent to the Registrar, but the change is not effective until the Registrar has advertised it in the *Gazette*.

COMPANIES HOUSE

353

Please complete in typescript,
or in bold black capitals.

Register of members

Company Number

Company Name in full

F353001R

The register of members is kept at:

NOTE:
The register **MUST** be kept at an address in the country of incorporation.

This notice is not required where the register has, at all times since it came into existence (or in the case of a register in existence on 1 July 1948 at all times since then) been kept at the registered office.

Address

Post town

County / Region

Postcode

Signed

Date

† Please delete as appropriate.

† a director / secretary / administrator / administrative receiver / receiver manager / receiver

Please give the name, address, telephone number and, if available, a DX number and Exchange of the person Companies House should contact if there is any query.

Tel

DX number

DX exchange

Companies House receipt date barcode

When you have completed and signed the form please send it to the Registrar of Companies at:
Companies House, Crown Way, Cardiff, CF4 3UZ   **DX 33050 Cardiff**
for companies registered in England and Wales
or
Companies House, 37 Castle Terrace, Edinburgh, EH1 2EB
for companies registered in Scotland   **DX 235 Edinburgh**

Form revised March 1995

Figure 6.3   Register of members

COMPANIES HOUSE

318

Please complete in typescript,
or in bold black capitals.

Location of directors' service contracts

Company Number

Company Name in full

✳F3180015✳

Address where directors' service contracts
or memoranda are available for inspection
by members.

NOTE:
Directors' service
contracts **MUST** be kept
at an address in the
country of incorporation.

This notice is not
required where the
relevant documents are
and have always been
kept at the Registered
Office.

Address

Post town

County / Region

Postcode

Signed

Date

† Please delete as appropriate.

† a director / secretary / administrator / administrative receiver / receiver manager / receiver

Please give the name, address,
telephone number and, if available,
a DX number and Exchange of
the person Companies House should
contact if there is any query.

Tel

DX number   DX exchange

When you have completed and signed the form please send it to the
Registrar of Companies at:
Companies House, Crown Way, Cardiff, CF4 3UZ   DX 33050 Cardiff
for companies registered in England and Wales
or
Companies House, 37 Castle Terrace, Edinburgh, EH1 2EB
for companies registered in Scotland   **DX 235 Edinburgh**

Form revised March 1995

Figure 6.4   Location of directors' service contracts

COMPANIES HOUSE

325

Please complete in typescript,
or in bold black capitals.

Location of register of directors' interests in shares etc.

Company Number

Company Name in full

F3250010

The register of directors' interests in shares and/or debentures is kept at:

NOTE:
The register MUST be
kept at an address in
the country of
incorporation.

This notice is not
required where the
register is and has
always been kept at the
Registered Office.

Address

Post town

County / Region

Postcode

Signed

Date

† Please delete as appropriate.

Please give the name, address,
telephone number and, if available,
a DX number and Exchange of
the person Companies House should
contact if there is any query.

† a director / secretary / administrator / administrative receiver / receiver manager / receiver

Tel

DX number   DX exchange

When you have completed and signed the form please send it to the
Registrar of Companies at:
Companies House, Crown Way, Cardiff, CF4 3UZ   **DX 33050 Cardiff**
for companies registered in England and Wales
or
Companies House, 37 Castle Terrace, Edinburgh, EH1 2EB
for companies registered in Scotland   **DX 235 Edinburgh**

Form revised March 1995

Figure 6.5   Location of register of directors' interests in shares, etc

G

COMPANIES FORM No.325a

Notice of place for inspection of a register of directors' interests in shares etc. which is kept in a non-legible form, or of any change in that place

325a

Please do not write in this margin

Pursuant to the Companies (Registers and Other Records) Regulations 1985

Note:For use only when the register is kept by computer or in some other non-legible form

Please complete legibly, preferably in black type, or bold block lettering

To the Registrar of Companies (Address overleaf)

For official use   Company number

Name of company

* insert full name of company

gives notice, in accordance with regulation 3(1) of the Companies (Registers and Other Records) Regulations 1985, that the place for inspection of the register of directors' interests in shares and/or debentures which the company keeps in a non-legible form is [now]†:

† delete as appropriate

Postcode

Signed   [Director][Secretary]† Date

Presentor's name address and reference (if any):

For official Use
General Section   Post room

Figure 6.6 Notice of place for inspection of a register of directors' interests in shares, etc, which is kept in a non-legible form, or of any change in that place

COMPANIES HOUSE

190

Please complete in typescript, or in bold black capitals.

Location of register of debenture holders

Company Number

Company Name in full

✱F1900010✱

gives notice that †[a register][registers]†[in duplicate form] of holders of debentures of the company of the classes mentioned below †[is][are]kept at:

NOTE:
This notice is not required where the register is, and has always been, kept at the Registered Office

Address

Post town

County / region

Postcode

Brief description of class of debentures

Signed

Date

† Please delete as appropriate.

† a director / secretary

Please give the name, address, telephone number and, if available, a DX number and Exchange of the person Companies House should contact if there is any query.

Tel

DX number   DX exchange

When you have completed and signed the form please send it to the Registrar of Companies at:
Companies House, Crown Way, Cardiff, CF4 3UZ   DX 33050 Cardiff
for companies registered in England and Wales
or
Companies House, 37 Castle Terrace, Edinburgh, EH1 2EB
for companies registered in Scotland   **DX 235 Edinburgh**

Form revised March 1995

Figure 6.7   Location of register of debenture holders

G

COMPANIES FORM No. 190a

Notice of place for inspection of a register of holders of debentures which is kept in a non-legible form, or of any change in that place

190a

Please do not write in this margin

Pursuant to the Companies (Registers and Other Records) Regulations 1985

Note: For use only when the register is kept by computer or in some other non-legible form

Please complete legibly, preferably in black type, or bold block lettering

To the Registrar of Companies (Address overleaf)

Name of company

For official use

Company number

* insert full name of company

*

gives notice, in accordance with regulation 5(1) of the Companies (Registers and Other Records) Regulations 1985, that the place for inspection of the register of debenture holders which the company keeps in a non-legible form is [now]:

Postcode

† delete as appropriate

Signed

[Director][Secretary]† Date

Presentor's name address and reference (if any) :

For official Use
General Section

Post room

Figure 6.8 Notice of place for inspection of a register of holders of debentures which is kept in a non-legible form, or of any change in that place

G

COMPANIES FORM No. 123

Notice of increase in nominal capital

123

CHWP000

Please do not write in this margin

Pursuant to section 123 of the Companies Act 1985

Please complete legibly, preferably in black type, or bold block lettering

To the Registrar of Companies **(Address overleaf)**

For official use

Company number

Name of company

* insert full name of company

*

gives notice in accordance with section 123 of the above Act that by resolution of the company

dated _____ the nominal capital of the company has been

increased by £ _____ beyond the registered capital of £ _____.

† the copy must be printed or in some other form approved by the registrar

A copy of the resolution authorising the increase is attached. †

The conditions (eg. voting rights, dividend rights, winding-up rights etc.) subject to which the new

shares have been or are to be issued are as follows :

Please tick here if continued overleaf

‡ Insert Director, Secretary, Administrator, Administrative Receiver or Receiver (Scotland) as appropriate

Signed

Designation ‡

Date

Presentor's name address and reference (if any) :

For official Use
General Section

Post room

Figure 6.9 Notice of increase in nominal capital

Companies House
— for the record —

CHWP000

Please complete in typescript, or
in bold black capitals.

88(2)

Return of Allotment of Shares

Company Number

Company name in full

Shares allotted (including bonus shares):

	From			To		
Date or period during which shares were allotted	Day	Month	Year	Day	Month	Year

(If shares were allotted on one date enter that date in the "from" box)

Class of shares
(ordinary or preference etc)

Number allotted

Nominal value of each share

Amount (if any) paid or due on each share (including any share premium)

List the names and addresses of the allottees and the number of shares allotted to each overleaf

If the allotted shares are fully or partly paid up otherwise than in cash please state:

% that each share is to be
treated as paid up

Consideration for which
the shares were allotted
(This information must be supported by
the duly stamped contract or by the duly
stamped particulars on Form 88(3) if the
contract is not in writing)

When you have completed and signed the form send it to the Registrar of Companies at:

Companies House receipt date barcode

This form has been provided free of charge by Companies House.

Companies House, Crown Way, Cardiff CF14 3UZ   DX 33050 Cardiff
For companies registered in England and Wales

Companies House, 37 Castle Terrace, Edinburgh EH1 2EB   DX 235 Edinburgh
For companies registered in Scotland

Form Revised January 2000

Figure 6.10   Return of allotment of shares

Companies House
— *for the record* —

6

Please complete in typescript, or in bold black capitals.
CHFP000

Cancellation of alteration to the objects of a company

Company Number

Company Name in full

An application was made to the Court on:

Day   Month   Year

for the cancellation of the alteration made to the objects of the company by a special resolution passed on:

Day   Month   Year

Signed   **Date**

† Please delete as appropriate.

† a director / secretary / administrator / administrative receiver / receiver manager / receiver

Please give the name, address, telephone number and, if available, a DX number and Exchange of the person Companies House should contact if there is any query.

Tel

DX number   DX exchange

Companies House receipt date barcode

This form has been provided free of charge by Companies House.

Form revised July 1998

When you have completed and signed the form please send it to the Registrar of Companies at:
Companies House, Crown Way, Cardiff, CF14 3UZ   **DX 33050 Cardiff**
for companies registered in England and Wales
or
Companies House, 37 Castle Terrace, Edinburgh, EH1 2EB
for companies registered in Scotland   **DX 235 Edinburgh**

Figure 6.11   Cancellation of alteration to the objects of a company

Changes in the Articles of Association

Alterations in the Articles are by a majority vote of the shareholders on a special resolution but if the company has two or more classes of shares, and the alteration affects the rights attached to any class, it should be done through a scheme of arrangement.

Printed and signed copies of resolutions altering the Articles must be sent to the Registrar within 15 days of the resolution but the alteration is not effective until the Registrar has advertised it in the *Gazette*.

Changing the accounting reference date

You can change the ARD by shortening or extending (to a maximum of 18 months) the accounting period (which fixes your accounting year). You can shorten the period as often and by as many months as you like. You cannot extend the period to more than 18 months from the start date and cannot extend it more than once in 5 years unless:

- the company is in adminstration;
- the Secretary of State has so directed; or
- the company is aligning its ARD with a subsidiary or parent undertaking in the EC.

The change must be made during a current period and details must be sent to the Registrar on *Form 225*. No time limit is specified but it must be sent before the end of the period.

Filing the accounts

Accounts must usually be filed 10 months after the ARD. If the company's first accounts cover a period of more than 12 months, however, they must be filed within 22 months of the date of incorporation. If the accounting reference period has been shortened the time allowed is 10 months or, if longer, 3 months from the date on *Form 225*.

For filing purposes a month after a specified date ends on the same date in the appropriate month, ie if the ARD is 30 October 2003, accounts must be filed before midnight on 30 August 2004. If there is no such date, eg the ARD ends on 30 April, accounts must be filed on the last day of the following February.

Extending the filing date

You can apply for a 3-month extension:

● If you carry on business or have interests abroad. *Form 244* must be delivered to Companies House before the normal filing deadline and filed for every year the company claims the extension.

● In special circumstances, eg if something beyond the company or the auditors' control delays the accounts. Written application must be made before the filing deadline, setting out the reasons for and the length of the required extension, to the Secretary of State for Trade and Industry. Companies incorporated in England and Wales apply c/o Companies Administration Section, Companies House, Cardiff. For Scottish companies the application is to Companies House, Edinburgh.

The *annual return* is sent to the Registrar on *Form 363a* (see page 83), signed by a director or the secretary. It must be made up to the 'return date', which is the anniversary of incorporation or, if the last return was made up to a different date, on the anniversary of that date.

Striking the company off the Register

Failure to file returns or accounts may lead to an enquiry as to whether the company has ceased trading and the Registrar may delete the company from the Register if:

● up-to-date information about the company's activities has not been filed; or

● there are no effective officers; or

● mail sent to the registered office is returned undelivered; or

● information is received that the company has ceased trading.

Before taking action the Registrar writes to the company to make enquiries. Failing a response, he then informs the company, and publishes notice in the *Gazette*, of his intention to strike the company off after three months unless cause is shown to the contrary. Before striking off, the Registrar considers the objections of creditors and may delay taking action in order to allow them to pursue their claims and to petition to wind up the company. Notice of striking off will then be published in the *Gazette*. If there are assets they are *bona vacantia*, that is, they belong to either the Crown or the Duchy of Lancaster or the Duchy of Cornwall, depending on the location of the registered office.

7

Insolvency

Limited liability means that if the business is insolvent, management's only liability is for fraud and for recklessness and incompetence which has jeopardised the interests of the creditors.

This chapter summarises the various procedures for winding up the company, but if drastic decisions must be made you should take expert advice. All the procedures require reference to, and action by, an insolvency practitioner, who must be a member of a recognised professional body such as the Institute of Chartered Accountants or the Law Society, or authorised by the Secretary of State. They involve formalities, meetings of shareholders and creditors, time limits, reporting to and filing documentation with the Registrar, and publicity; there are fines and penalties if you do not comply with the statutory requirements.

What is insolvency?

A company is legally insolvent if it is unable to pay its debts and discharge its liabilities as and when they fall due, or the value of its assets is less than its liabilities. In determining liabilities, contingent and prospective liabilities must be taken into account, as well as actual and quantified amounts. Day-to-day involvement in management often gives a false picture of the company's financial position and if customers are slow to pay, plant, machinery and stock have been purchased under credit agreements and the company's bank account is in overdraft, the business may be far from healthy, however heavy the order book. Financial problems need not, however, lead to liquidation. The procedures introduced by the 1986 Insolvency Act permit a company to reach a compromise agreement with creditors, or to apply to the court for an administration order, so that company affairs can be reorganised and supervised and insolvency avoided.

You should therefore ensure that you have adequate accounting records and proper financial advice so that you are able to consider taking appropriate action.

Voluntary striking off

If a company has effectively ceased to operate, the Registrar may consider a written request to strike the company off the Register. If the company is struck off, any remaining assets pass to the Crown, the Duchy of Lancaster or the Duchy of Cornwall, depending on the location of the registered office. If there are debts, the creditors can object and, in any event, the directors', management's and shareholders' liability continues as if the company had not been dissolved.

Voluntary arrangements: compositions and schemes of arrangement

Arrangements with creditors

These procedures offer a relatively straightforward method whereby a potentially solvent company concludes a legally effective arrangement with creditors with minimum reference to the court.

Procedure

The directors or the liquidator or administrator (see below) put a statement of affairs – which sets out the company's financial position – and detailed proposals to creditors and shareholders for a *scheme* or *composition* in satisfaction of debts. They must nominate an insolvency practitioner to supervise the arrangement and, unless he is a liquidator or administrator, he must report to the court as to the necessity for shareholders' and creditors' meetings and notify creditors. A liquidator or administrator must call meetings but need not report to court. The meetings must approve the supervisor and can accept, modify or reject the proposals. Secured and preferred creditors are protected; directors, shareholders, creditors and the supervisor can challenge decisions and implementation.

The arrangement is carried out by the supervisor and he or she can refer to the court, which can stay (stop) the winding up and discharge an administration order.

Administration orders

This procedure is mainly for companies which do not borrow on standard fixed and floating charges and enables a potentially or actually insolvent company to put its affairs in the hands of an administrator, so that part or all of the company can be salvaged or a more advantageous realisation of assets can be secured than on a winding up.

Application is made to the court, which must be satisfied that the company is, or is likely to become, unable to pay its debts. In addition, the court must consider that the order would be likely to enable part or all of the undertaking to survive as a going concern, and/or creditors are likely to agree a satisfactory arrangement with the company, and/or realisation of the assets is likely to be more advantageous than if the company were wound up.

The order can be used together with a voluntary arrangement or compromise or arrangement with creditors under the Companies Acts but not if the company is already in liquidation.

The petition is presented to the court by the company and/or directors and/or creditors and notice must be given to debenture holders who have appointed, or have the right to appoint, an administrative receiver under a floating charge. On presentation of the petition, the administrator takes over management and no legal proceedings can issue or continue against the company, but an administrative receiver can be appointed and a petition for winding up can be presented. A more detailed statement of affairs verifed on affidavit by current and former officers of the company and, in some circumstances, employees, is drawn up and the administrator's proposals for reorganisation, which depend on the terms of the court order, can be rejected by shareholders, creditors or the court although the creditors' approval is not mandatory.

Receivership

This is the procedure by which assets secured by a floating charge are realised. Secured creditors can enforce their security independently of a winding up and without regard to the unsecured creditors or to the interests of the company.

Administrative receivers are appointed under a debenture secured by a charge and the appointment can be over all or a substantial part of the company's assets. The appointment can be by the debenture holders or the court, and again the administrative receiver takes over management.

Receivers are appointed under the terms of a fixed charge or by the court but they cannot act as administrative receivers. Their powers depend on the terms of the charge or court order and the appointment suspends the fixed charge holders' right to enforce their security without the consent of the court or administrator, who can dispose of the charged property, giving them the same priority as they would have had if they had enforced the charge directly.

Receivers and directors

The directors' powers effectively cease when a receiver or administrative receiver is appointed. A receiver ceases to act when he has sufficient funds to discharge the debt due to his appointor and his expenses but an administrative receiver can only be removed by court order.

Voluntary arrangement

There have been frequent complaints that secured creditors, particularly banks, act primarily in their own interests and ignore the interests of other creditors and the company.

With some exceptions appointing an administrative receiver has now been barred under charges created on or after 20 June 2003. Instead, securities must be enforced through the appointment of an administrator who owes a duty and has to account to all the company's creditors.

The appointment can still be made by the Court, but holders of a floating charge can on 2 days' notice, or the company or its directors on 5 days' notice, choose instead to file a notice of appointment with the court. No reports have to be filed explaining why the company should go into administration, although the company or the directors (but not the floating charge-holder) must file a statement that the company is or is likely to become unable to pay its debts, and that the administrator believes that the purpose of administration is reasonably likely to be achieved.

The administrator then takes over management of the company to:

● rescue the company as a going concern; or
● achieve a better result for the creditors as a whole than would be likely if the company were wound up without first going into administration; or
● realise the assets in order to make a distribution to the secured or preferential creditors.

Time limits have been shortened and there is an overall time limit of one year for the process of administration, with an extension of six months with the creditors' consent or longer if the court so orders. If the administrator is unable to rescue the company, he must file a notice with the court converting to a creditors' voluntary liquidation and he acts as liquidator unless the creditors decide otherwise.

Protection for floating charge-holders

The floating charge-holder can choose his own administrator even if there is already an application before the court, unless the court decides otherwise and can also apply for the appointment of an administrator if the company is in compulsory liquidation.

Voluntary arrangement with a moratorium

This new scheme requires proposals for a voluntary arrangement being put to the company by a nominated insolvency practitioner, who calls shareholders' and creditors' meetings to approve the voluntary arrangement and on approval supervises the arrangement. When the proposals are drawn up and supported by the nominee the directors can obtain a 28 day moratorium (which stops creditors and others from enforcing their legal remedies) by filing the terms of the proposals and certain other documents with the court. There must be both creditors' and shareholders' meetings, the moratorium must be advertised and the registrar notified. The 28-day period can be shortened and, with the creditors' consent, extended by 2 months.

During the moratorium the nominee monitors the company's affairs and the directors cannot act without his consent. The moratorium ends with the calling of the required meetings that either approve or reject the voluntary arrangement. If there is disagreement, the decision of the creditors' meeting is decisive.

Procedurally this is more complicated and public than a voluntary arrangement. There are more constraints on the directors and it is likely to be more costly because of the increased involvement of the insolvency practitioner.

Winding up

This is the statutory procedure which brings a company's operations to an end, realising the assets and distributing the proceeds among creditors and shareholders in accordance with their rights. The company is then dissolved.

A company can be wound up compulsorily by court order or voluntarily by the shareholders if it is insolvent, or by shareholders if it is solvent.

Voluntary winding up

The company puts itself into voluntary liquidation by passing a resolution at a general meeting of the shareholders. Seven days' notice of the meeting must be given and a notice of a creditors' meeting to be held on the same day or the day after must be sent on the same date. The decision can be by ordinary resolution if the company was formed for a fixed period or a specific undertaking; otherwise a special resolution must be passed. An extraordinary resolution is necessary if the company is insolvent.

Voluntary liquidation

A members' or shareholders' voluntary liquidation requires the majority of the directors to prepare a declaration of solvency after full enquiry into the company's affairs. The declaration sets out the company's assets and liabilities and states that it will be able to pay its debts within, at most, 12 months; if they are not paid, the directors may be liable to a fine or imprisonment.

If no declaration is made or the liquidator disagrees with its conclusion or the company cannot pay its debts within 12 months, it becomes a creditors' voluntary liquidation and the creditors appoint and can supervise the liquidator.

The advantage of a voluntary liquidation is that, although employees are dismissed if the company is insolvent, the directors can continue to act provided they have the approval of the liquidator and of the shareholders given in general meeting; in a creditors' voluntary liquidation the creditors must also give their consent.

If the resolution is passed without appointing a liquidator, the directors can dispose of perishable goods and those likely to diminish in value unless immediately disposed of, and take action necessary to protect company assets until one is appointed. Any further action requires the consent of the court, and the company must stop trading except in so far as may be required for beneficial winding up.

The liquidation starts on the date the resolution for winding up is passed; if the liquidator thinks the company is insolvent, the winding up continues as a creditors' voluntary liquidation. The liquidator stays in office until removed after his final report to shareholders and creditors but he can resign or vacate office on notice to the Registrar of the final meeting.

Distribution

Available assets are applied against the company's liabilities, and shareholders are only called on for any balance remaining unpaid on their shares.

Creditors' rights

Fixed chargeholders take the first slice of the assets, followed by liquidation expenses, preferential debts, floating chargeholders and sums due to shareholders (for instance, arrears of dividend), although in some circumstances floating chargeholders may have prior claims to holders of a fixed charge. Remaining assets go to unsecured creditors, who can claim interest to the date of distribution, and any surplus is divided among shareholders in accordance with their rights under the Memorandum and Articles of Association.

Preferential debts comprise outstanding tax to a maximum of 12 months, including PAYE; contributions in respect of subcontractors in the construction industry; six months' VAT; general betting duty; 12 months' National Insurance contributions; state and occupational pension scheme contributions; arrears of wages for four months (including directors but not the managing director) to a maximum of £240 per week, including Statutory Sick Pay, protective awards, payment during medical suspension, time off work and accrued holiday pay. Wages Act employee claims are paid if the company has more than ten employees and most amounts payable to employees under the employment legislation can be reimbursed partly or wholly from the Redundancy Fund. Employees can claim for any balance still outstanding with the ordinary (unsecured) creditors.

Dissolution in a voluntary liquidation

The company is dissolved three months from registration by the Registrar of the liquidator's final account and return.

Compulsory winding up

The compulsory procedure can be initiated by the company, a shareholder, a creditor, the official receiver (employed by the Department of Trade and Industry), or the Department of Trade and Industry.

The most frequent basis for the petition is insolvency, which here is presumed if a creditor has been owed at least £750 for more than three weeks after a formal demand has been served, or the company has not discharged a judgment debt or court order. The court appoints a liquidator who can, without reference to the court or creditors, take over management of the company forthwith. Here the liquidator not only gets in and distributes the assets but also must provide the official receiver with any information and documents he or she requires. The official receiver must look into the cause of the company's failure, reporting if necessary to the court, and he or she can apply for public examination of officers, liquidators, administrators and anyone else involved in the company's affairs.

Fines and penalties

If the company has been trading with an intent to defraud creditors or anyone else, or incurring debts without a reasonable prospect of repayment, anyone involved may be prosecuted and disqualified from participating directly or indirectly in the management of a company for a maximum of 15 years. Conviction for an indictable offence (that is, a serious offence triable by jury in the Crown Court) relating to the promotion, formation, management or liquidation of a company, or with the receivership or management of its property, or for persistent failure to file accounts and records, can also lead to disqualification.

Fraudulent and wrongful trading can in addition bring a personal liability for all the company's debts. Fraudulent trading is trading with an intent to defraud creditors and, if the company is in insolvent liquidation and a director, *de facto*, or shadow director knew, or should have known, that there was no reasonable prospect that the company could have avoided insolvent liquidation, there may also be criminal liability for wrongful trading and disqualification.

Officers of the company and anyone else acting in the promotion, formation, management or liquidation of a company in liquidation are personally liable if they retain or misapply assets or they are in breach of duty to the company.

Voidable transactions: preferences and transactions at an undervalue

Any transaction entered into by an insolvent company which puts a creditor, surety or guarantor into a better position than he would be in the liquidation may be voidable and set aside as a (fraudulent) 'preference'. The preference may be a transaction at a proper price or at an undervalue (that is, a gratuitous gift or transfer or one made for significantly less than market value). The risk period dates back from presentation of a petition for an administrative order or the date the order is made, or the commencement of liquidation.

Transactions at a proper price or an undervalue are safe if made in good faith and for the purpose of carrying on the business, provided that at the time there were reasonable grounds that the transaction would benefit the company. They are at risk, however, if made at a time when the company was unable to pay its debts or it became unable to pay them as a result of the transaction. Preferences at an undervalue and any preference, even one at a proper price, with a connected person is at risk for two years; there is a six-month risk period for other preferences and preferences made in the period prior to the making of an administration order.

The network of connected persons here extends to cover directors, shadow directors (persons in accordance with whose instructions directors are accustomed to act), company officers and their spouses, including a former and reputed spouse, and their children and step-children, as well as their partners, a company with which they are associated and of which they control at lease one-fifth of the voting shares and a trustee of any trust under which they, their family group, or associated company is a beneficiary.

Floating charges may also be voidable. They are valid whenever created to the extent that consideration (that is, payment in cash, goods or services or in discharge of debts) is received by the company. The balance is at risk for one year if made when the company was unable to pay its debts, and two years if made in favour of a connected person.

Distribution is on the same basis as in voluntary liquidation.

Dissolution in compulsory winding up

The liquidator reports to a final meeting of creditors when winding up is completed; if the official receiver is acting, he can apply for early dissolution on the basis that assets will not cover winding up expenses and no further investigation is required. Three months from the date of registration of dissolution entered by the Registrar, the company is dissolved.

Restriction on use of the company name

Directors and shadow directors acting within 12 months of insolvent liquidation cannot act for, or be involved with, a company with the same name.
Nor can they for five years use a former name or trading name used during
the previous 12 months or one so similar as to suggest continuing association, without the consent of the court. Non-compliance brings a personal
joint and several liability with the company and anyone acting on the
offender's instructions.

8 *The ready-made company*

The fastest way to incorporation is to buy an 'off the shelf', ready-made company already registered at Companies House from your solicitor or accountant or one of the many registration agents who advertise in financial and professional journals and the Yellow Page All the necessary documentation will have been filed with the Registrar and the company will have a Certificate of Incorporation, so that it can start trading as soon as you have appointed your own director(s) and secretary and transferred the shares to your own shareholders.

Your solicitor or accountant can incorporate your company through a company agent's fast-track electronic filing service at a cost of £50 to £150. If you use agents, you are advised to use members of the Association of Company Registration Agents, and if you want to choose your own company name they will check its availability for a fee. If you intend to use the name as a trade mark, you should also carry out a search at the Trade Marks Registry in the appropriate class of goods and services.

Companies House will send you information packs and guides and agents will advise you on the necessary initial changes for takeover. The objects clause can be changed but you should ensure that the existing principal objects clause covers your main business activities.

You will then have a company with a current Certificate of Incorporation, a standard Memorandum of Association with an appropriate objects and capital clause, standard Articles of Association, a set of statutory books and a company seal if this is required by your Articles, for a cost of about £150 including VAT. The existing directors, secretary and shareholders of the ready-made company, usually the agent's nominees, resign in favour of your nominees.

If the nominee shareholders were companies, your ready-made company cannot claim exemption from audit for its accounts (see page 90), unless it is dormant throughout its first financial year. It may therefore be worthwhile shortening the first accounting period so it ends on the day on which you take ownership of the shares (see page 82). The company must, however, pass a special resolution not to appoint auditors and deliver dormant company accounts for the first (shortened) period, before the first general meeting at which accounts are laid.

You may wish to make other changes, which must be notified to the Registrar of Companies in accordance with the Companies Act and which are dealt with in Chapter 6. These involve some delay but the procedure is more straightforward and less expensive than starting from scratch.

There are a number of nationally recognised formations' (or registration) agents including, in alphabetical order: 4 Business, Al, Jordans, London Law, Stanley Davis, York Place and Waterlows.

Appendix 1

Notes for guidance on company names

A. Use of the following words and expressions in a company or business name requires the prior approval of the Secretary of State for Trade and Industry:

(a) *Words that imply national or international pre-eminence*

International	British	Wales
National	England	Welsh
European	English	Ireland
United Kingdom	Scotland	Irish
Great Britain	Scottish	

(b) *Words that imply business pre-eminence or representative or authoritative status*

Association	Authority	Board
Council	Federation	Institute
Institution	Society	

(c) *Words that imply specific objects or functions*

Assurance	Chamber of Commerce,	Building Society
Insurance	Training and Enterprise	Chemist
Trade Union	Reinsurance	Chemistry
Foundation	Reassurance	Group
Fund	Insurer	Holding
Charity	Assurer	Post Office
Charter	Reassurer	Register
Chartered	Reinsurer	Registered
Cooperative	Patent	Friendly Society
Stock Exchange	Patentee	
Trust	Chamber of Trade	

Benevolent   Chamber of Industry
Sheffield

B. Use of the following words and expressions also requires the prior consent of the relevant body as well as the Secretary of State. A statement that a written request has been made to the relevant body seeking its opinion as to use of the word or expression must be filed with the application for registration, together with a copy of any response:

Word or expression	*Relevant body for persons intending to set up business in England or Wales*	*Relevant body for persons intending to set up business in Scotland*
Royal, Royale, Royalty, King, Queen, Prince, Princess, Windsor, Duke, His/ Her Majesty	Lord Chancellors Department Constitutional Policy Division, 1st Floor, Southside, 105 Victoria Street, London SW1E 6QT (if based in England) The National Assembly for Wales Cathays Park, Cardiff CF1 3NQ (if based in Wales)	The Scottish Minister's Civil Law and LA Division Saughton House, Broomhouse Drive, Edinburgh EH11 3XD
Police	Home Office Police Dept Strategy Group, Room 510, 50 Queen Anne's Gate, London SW1H 9AT	The Scottish Minister's Police Division 50 Andrew's House, Regent Road, Edinburgh EH1 3DQ
Special School	Department for Education and Employment, Schools 2 Branch, Sanctuary Buildings, Gt Smith St, London SW1P 3BT	As for England & Wales
Contact Lens	General Optical Council, 37 Wimpole Street, London W1M 8DQ	As for England & Wales

District Nurse, Health Visitor, Midwife, Midwifery, Health Visiting, Nurse, Nursing	United Kingdom Central Council for Nursing and Midwifery 23 Portland Place, London W1N 3AF	As for England & Wales
Health Centre	Office of the Solicitor Department of Health and Social Security 48 Carey Street, London WC2A 2LS	As for England & Wales
Health Service	Department of Health, NHS Management Wellington House, 133–135 Waterloo Road, London SE1 8UG	As for England & Wales
Pregnancy, Termination, Abortion	Department of Health, Area 423, Wellington House 133–155 Waterloo Road, London SE1 8UG	As for England & Wales
Charity, Charitable	Charity Commission, Registration Division, Harmsworth House, 13–15 Bouverie Street, London EC4Y 8DP	Inland Revenue, Claims Branch, Trinity Park House, South Trinity Road, Edinburgh EH5 3SD
or for companies NOT intending to register as a charity	Charity Commission, 2nd Floor, 20 Kings Parade, Queens Dock, Liverpool L3 4DQ	
Apothecary	The Worshipful Society of Apothecaries of London, Apothecaries Hall, Blackfriars Lane, London EC4V 6EJ	The Pharmaceutical Society of Great Britain, Law Department, 1 Lambeth High Street, London SE1 7JN

Polytechnic	Department for Education and Science, FHE 1B Sanctuary Buildings, Great Smith St, London SW1P 3BT	As for England & Wales
University	Privy Council Office 2 Carlton Gardens, London SW1Y 5AA	As for England & Wales

C. The use of certain words is covered by other legislation and may constitute a criminal offence. Some of these words are listed below but the list is not exhaustive. If you wish to use any of them, you should seek legal advice and confirmation from the body concerned that the use of the word does not contravene the relevant legislation, but their opinion is not conclusive:

Word or expression	Relevant legislation	Relevant body
Architect, Architectural	Section 1 Architects Registration Registration Act 1997	Architects Registration Board 73 Hallan Street London
Chiropodist, Dietician, Medical Laboratory, Technician, Occupational Therapist, Orthoptist, Physiotherapist, Radiographer, Remedial Gymnast, professions supplementary to Medicine Act 1960 if preceded by Registered, State or State Registered	Medicine Act 1960	Department of Health HRD HRB Room 2N35A Quarry House Quarry Hill Leeds LS2 7JE
Credit Union	Credit Union Act 1979	The Public Records Section Financial Service Authority 25 The North Colonnade Canary Wharf, London E14 5HS

| | | Scottish Association Registrars of Friendly Societies, 58 Frederick St, Edinburgh EH2 1NB |

Dentist, Dental Surgeon, Dental Practitioner, Dentistry	Dental Act 1984	General Dental Council, 37 Wimpole St, London W1M 8DQ
Veterinary Surgeon, Veterinary, Vet	Sections 19/20 Veterinary Surgeons Act 1966	Royal College of Veterinary Surgeons, Belgravia House, 62–64 Horseferry Road, London SW1P 2AF
Pharmaceutical Drug, Druggist, Pharmaceutical Pharmaceutist, Pharmacist, Pharmacy	Section 78 Medicines Act 1968	The Director of Legal Services The Royal Society of Great Britain, 1 Lambeth High St, London SE1 7JN Scotland: The Pharmaceutical Society 36 York Place Edinburgh EH13
Red Cross, Geneva Cross, Red Crescent, Red Lion and Sun	Geneva Convention Act 1957	Seek advice of Companies House
Anzac	Anzac Act 1916	Seek advice of Companies House
Inst of Laryngology, Inst of Otology, Inst of Utology, Inst of Orthopaedics	University College of London Act 1988	Seek advice of University College, Gower Street, London WC1E 6BT
Olympiad, Olympiads, Olympian, Olympians, Olympic, Olympics, or translation of these	Olympic Symbol etc (Protection) Act 1995*	Olympic Association 1 Wandsworth Plain London SW18 1EH

*Also protects Olympic symbols of five interlocking rings and motto '*Citius Altius Fortius*'

Patent Office, Patent Agent	Copyright Design & Patents Act 1988	IPDD, Room 3B38, Concept House, The Patent Office, Cardiff Road, Newport NP10 8QQ
Building Society	Building Society Act 1986	Seek advice of Building Societies Commission, Victoria House, 30–40 Kingsway, London WC2B 6ES
Chamber(s) of Business, Chamber(s) of Commerce, Chamber(s) of Commerce & Industry, Chamber(s) of Commerce, Training & Enterprise Chamber(s) of Enterprise Chamber(s) of Industry Chamber(s) of Trade Chamber(s) of Trade and Industry, Chamber(s) of Training Chamber(s) of Training and Enterprise or Welsh translations of these words	Company & Business Names (Chamber of Commerce etc) Act 1999	Guidance available from Companies House

Only persons carrying on business as a building society in the UK may use a name which implies that they are in any way connected with the business of a building society.

D. 'Too like' names – The Secretary of State takes account of facts which might suggest similarity and lead to confusion including, for instance, the nature and location of a business. Evidence to show confusion is taken into account.

E. A name suggesting a connection with a company already on the Index – The Secretary of State does not consider 'implied association' – ie whether the company might be thought to be a member of, or associated with, another company or group. Nor is consideration given to trading names, logos, trade or service marks, copyrights, patents, etc or any other proprietary rights existing in names or parts of names.

F.   Company letterhead – Business owned by a company:

Bert's Shoes

6 Tuppeny Passage, London NW12 5TT

Bert's Shoes (UK) Limited
Registered in England and Wales
Registration Number: 123456789
Registered Office, 81 Florin Way, London NW13 7DD

The restrictions applying to business names are similar to those applying to company names.

Information required to be disclosed by the Business Names Act 1985 and the Companies Act 1985.

Appendix 2

Documents to be filed on incorporation by a private limited liability company

1. MEMORANDUM OF ASSOCIATION, stating the company's name, the situation of its registered office (England, Scotland or Wales), the objects for which the company is formed and the powers taken by the company, that the liability of the shareholders is limited and the amount of the share capital divided into shares of a fixed amount. It must be dated and subscribed by not less than two persons (the subscribers), their signatures duly witnessed.

2. ARTICLES OF ASSOCIATION (unless Table A (see page 22) is adopted), setting out the regulations governing the company's internal affairs. This must be printed, dated and signed by the subscribers to the Memorandum and their signatures duly witnessed.

3. Statement of First Directors and Secretary and Intended Situation of Registered Office (Form 10). The form can be signed by the subscribers to the Memorandum or by agents acting on their behalf and sets out the prescribed details of the directors and secretary, who must also sign the form confirming their consent to act.

4. Declaration of Compliance with the Requirements on Application for Registration of a Company (Form 12). This can be made by a director or secretary named in the Statement of first officers above or by a solicitor engaged in the company's formation.

Appendix 3

Documents which must be lodged with the Registrar*

Document	Form	Signatories	When lodged	Penalty
Statement of first directors secretary and intended situation of registered office	10	Subscribers or their agent and each officer	Before registration	None
Declaration of compliance with requirements on application for registration	12	Director, secretary or solicitor acting	ditto	None
Notice of change of registered office	287	Director or secretary	Within 14 days of change	£400 + £40 daily
Notice of change directors, secretary or in their particulars	288	ditto	ditto	£2,000 + £200 daily

* The documentation listed covers the more straightforward company business. It does not include documentation which must be filed when you are involved in transactions requiring specialist legal and/or accountancy advice, for instance where application has been made to the court to vary shareholders' rights or to reduce the company's share capital.

Document	Form	Signatories	When lodged	Penalty
Contract constituting allottees' title to shares and contract of sale	–	All parties to contract	Within 14 days of change	£2,000 + £200 daily
Particulars of contract re shares allotted as fully or partly paid up otherwise than in cash	88(3)	Director or secretary	Within 1 month of allotment of shares for non-cash consideration (used when no written contract)	ditto
Return of allotment of shares	88(2)	ditto	Within 1 month of allotment	No limit on indictment. £2,000 on summary conviction + £200 daily
(first) Notice of accounting reference date	224	ditto	Within 9 months of incorporation	None but date is then 31/3
Notice of new accounting reference date	225	ditto	Before end of period	None but change ineffective
Accounts	225	Director	Within 10 months of accounting reference period	£100 to £1,000 depending on delay
Annual return	363a	Director or secretary	Within 28 days of the return date	£2,000 + £200 daily
Special resolution	–	Director, secretary or chairman of meeting	Within 15 days of passing resolution	£1,000 + £40 daily

Extraordinary resolution	–	Director, secretary or chairman of meeting	Within 15 days of passing resolution	£400 + £40 daily
Other resolution or agreement by all members or class of members not otherwise effective unless passed as special or extraordinary resolution	–	ditto	ditto	ditto
Resolution authorising increase of share capital	–	ditto	ditto	ditto
Notice of increase in nominal capital	123	Director or secretary	ditto	ditto
Notice of passing of resolution removing an auditor	386	ditto	Within 14 days of passing resolution	ditto
Notice of place where copies of director's service contracts kept or of change in place	318	ditto	Within 14 days	ditto
Notice of place where register of members kept or of change in place	353	ditto	ditto	ditto

Notice of place where register of holders of debentures or duplicate kept or of change in place	190	ditto	Not specified	Not specified
Notice of place where register of directors' interests in shares etc kept or of change in place	325	Director or secretary	Within 14 days daily	£400 + £40 daily
Particulars of mortgage or charge	395	Director, secretary, solicitor to company or mortgagee	Within 21 days of creation (instrument also to be produced)	No limit on conviction on indictment. £2,000 on summary conviction + £200 daily
Particulars for registration of charge to secure series of debentures	397	Director, secretary, solicitor to company or debenture holder or their solicitor	Within 21 days of execution of trust deed or debentures (if no deed) and the deed or one debenture	ditto
Particulars of a mortgage or charge subject to which property has been acquired	400	Director or secretary	Within 21 days of acquisition	ditto
Declaration of satisfaction in full or in part of mortgage or charge	403a	Under company seal at company's option but best attested as required by articles	lodged forthwith	ditto

Declaration that part of property or undertaking (a) has been released from charge; (b) no longer forms part of undertaking	403b	Under company seal attested as required by articles	At company's option but best lodged forthwith	No limit on conviction on indictment. £2,000 on summary conviction + £200 daily.
Notice of appointment receiver or manager	405(1)*	Person obtaining order or making appointment or their solicitor	Within 7 days of court order or appointment	£400 + £40 daily
Notice of ceasing to act as receiver or manager	405(2)*	Receiver or manager	On ceasing to act	ditto
Printed copy of memorandum as altered by special resolution	–	–	Within 15 days after period for making application to court for cancelling alteration	ditto

*Not illustrated

Note: Documents sent to Companies House are microfilmed; forms should therefore be completed legibly and in black ink. Typed documents should be on A4 paper with a margin of not less than 10 millimetres (20 millimetres if documents are bound). Computer print is acceptable but dot matrix and carbon copy documents are not.

Accompanying cheques should be made payable to Companies House.

Fees for inspection, copies and extracts
Companies House provides public records of information filed by companies on paper, microfiche, roll film and magnetic tape and via e-mail, fax (ordered by credit/debit card) and courier as well as via database direct to your PC. Credit card customers and account holders can only order by telephone, and credit card orders are subject to a minimum charge of £5.

The following company details are available free of charge on the Companies House Web site at www.companieshouse.gov.uk:

- company indexes;
- basic company details;
- a history of company transactions;
- the register of disqualified directors;
- insolvency details.

There is a charge of £1–4.00 for viewing company documents online and they can be downloaded for £3.00. Payment is by credit card with a minimum charge of £5.00.

Charges for paper documents ordered by post or telephone start at £4.00, copies by fax are £3.00 and by e-mail, £2.50.

Companies House also provides bulk compilations, including company analysis list by VAT trade classification, postcode, incorporation date or company status and a Register of Directors, Register of Registered Charges and New Incorporation Prints. More detailed analysis of the information held by Companies House is available on request.

High volume users, for instance, company formation agents, can use the electronic incorporation service but otherwise filing is by post, Document Exchange or courier. Faxed copies of statutory documents are not accepted for registration. Acknowledgement of receipt of documents is only given if postage or carriage is pre-paid.

Enquiries can be made by e-mail to enquiries@companieshjouse.gov.uk and by telephone to 0870 333 3636 or fax to 02920 380517.

10

Please complete in typescript, or in bold black capitals.
CHWP000
Notes on completion appear on final page

First directors and secretary and intended situation of registered office

Company Name in full

Proposed Registered Office
(PO Box numbers only, are not acceptable)

Post town

County / Region

Postcode

If the memorandum is delivered by an agent for the subscriber(s) of the memorandum mark the box opposite and give the agent's name and address.

Agent's Name

Address

Post town

County / Region

Postcode

Number of continuation sheets attached

You do not have to give any contact information in the box opposite but if you do, it will help Companies House to contact you if there is a query on the form. The contact information that you give will be visible to searchers of the public record.

Tel

DX number   DX exchange

Companies House receipt date barcode
This form is been provided free of charge by Companies House

v 08/02

When you have completed and signed the form please send it to the Registrar of Companies at:
Companies House, Crown Way, Cardiff, CF14 3UZ   DX 33050 Cardiff
for companies registered in England and Wales
or
Companies House, 37 Castle Terrace, Edinburgh, EH1 2EB
for companies registered in Scotland   **DX 235 Edinburgh**

Figure A3.1   Statement of rights attached to allotted shares

G

COMPANIES FORM No. 128(3)

**Statement of particulars of
variation of rights attached
to shares**

128(3)

Please do not
write in
this margin

Pursuant to section 128(3) of the Companies Act 1985

Please complete
legibly, preferably
in block type, or
bold block lettering

To the Registrar of Companies
(Address overleaf)

For official use

Company number

Name of company

* insert full name
of company

*

§ insert date

On §_____ the rights attached to

Number of Shares	Class(es) of share

were varied as set out below (otherwise than by amendment of the company's memorandum or

articles or by any resolution or agreement to which section 380 of the above Act applies)

‡ Insert
Director,
Secretary,
Administrator,
Administrative
Receiver or
Receiver
(Scotland) as
appropriate

Signed   Designation‡   Date

Presentor's name address and
reference (if any):

For official Use
General Section   Post room

Figure A3.2   Statement of particulars of variation of rights attached to
shares

G

COMPANIES FORM No. 128(4)

Notice of assignment of name or new name to any class of shares

128(4)

Pursuant to section 128(4) of the Companies Act 1985

To the Registrar of Companies

For official use

Company number

Name of company

*

gives notice of the assignment of a [new]† name or other designation to the following class[es]† of shares (otherwise than by amendment of the company's memorandum or articles or by any resolution or agreement to which section 380 of the above Act applies)

Number and class of shares	Name or other designation

Signed   Designation‡   Date

Presentor's name address and reference (if any):

For official Use

General Section   Post room

Figure A3.3   Notice of assignment of name or new name to any class of shares

G

COMPANIES FORM No.155(6)a

Declaration in relation to assistance for the acquisition of shares.

155(6)a

Pursuant to section 155(6) of the Companies Act 1985

To the Registrar of Companies
(Address overleaf- Note 5)

For official use

Company number

Name of company

*

I/We ø _____

_____

_____

_____

_____

_____

_____

[the sole director][all the directors]† of the above company do solemnly and sincerely declare that:

The business of the company is:

(a) that of a [recognised bank][licensed institution]† within the meaning of the Banking Act 1979§

(b) that of a person authorised under section 3 or 4 of the Insurance Companies Act 1982 to carry on insurance business in the United Kingdom§

(c) something other than the above§

The company is proposing to give financial assistance in connection with the acquisition of shares in the [company] [company's holding company _____

_____ Limited]†

The assistance is for the purpose of [that acquisition][reducing or discharging a liability incurred for the purpose of that acquisition].†

The number and class of the shares acquired or to be acquired is: _____

_____

Presentor's name address and reference (if any):

For official Use

General Section

Post room

Page 1

Figure A3.4   Declaration in relation to assistance for the acquisition of shares

The assistance is to be given to: (note 2) _____

Please do not write in this margin

Please complete legibly, preferably in block type, or bold block lettering

The assistance will take the form of:

The person who [has acquired][will acquire]† the shares is:

† delete as appropriate

The principal terms on which the assistance will be given are:

The amount of cash to be transferred to the person assisted is £ _____

The value of any asset to be transferred to the person assisted is £ _____

The date on which the assistance is to be given is _____ 19 _____

Page 2

Figure A3.4 *continued*

Please do not
write in
this margin

Please complete
legibly, preferably
in black type, or
bold block lettering

* delete either (a) or
(b) as appropriate

I/We have formed the opinion, as regards the company's initial situation immediately following the date on which the assistance is proposed to be given, that there will be no ground on which it could then be found to be unable to pay its debts.(note 3)

(a)[I/We have formed the opinion that the company will be able to pay its debts as they fall due during the year immediately following that date]*(note 3)

(b)[It is intended to commence the winding-up of the company within 12 months of that date, and I/we have formed the opinion that the company will be able to pay its debts in full within 12 months of the commencement of the winding up.]*(note 3)

And I/we make this solemn declaration conscientiously believing the same to be true and by virtue of the provisions of the Statutory Declarations Act 1835.

Declared at _____   Declarants to sign below

_____

the _____ day of _____

Two thousand and_____

_____

before me _____

A Commissioner for Oaths or Notary Public or Justice of
the Peace or a Solicitor having the powers conferred on
a Commissioner for Oaths.

NOTES

1 For the meaning of "a person incurring a
liability" and "reducing or discharging a
liability" see section 152(3) of the Companies
Act 1985.

2 Insert full name(s) and address(es) of the
person(s) to whom assistance is to be given; if
a recipient is a company the registered office
address should be shown.

3 Contingent and prospective liabilities of the
company are to be taken into account - see
section 156(3) of the Companies Act 1985

4 The auditors report required by section 156(4)
of the Companies Act 1985 must be annexed
to this form.

5 The address for companies registered in
England and Wales or Wales is:-

The Registrar of Companies
Companies House
Crown Way
Cardiff
CF4 3UZ

or, for companies registered in Scotland:-

The Registrar of Companies
Companies House
100-102 George Street
Edinburgh
EH2 3DJ

Page 3

Figure A3.4   *continued*

G

COMPANIES FORM No. 169

Return by a company purchasing its own shares

169

Pursuant to section 169 of the Companies Act 1985

Please do not write in this margin

Please complete legibly, preferably in black type, or bold block lettering

To the Registrar of Companies
(Address overleaf)

Please do not write in the space below. For Inland Revenue use only.

For official use

Company number

* insert full name of company

Name of company

*

Note
This return must be delivered to the Registrar within a period of 28 days beginning with the first date on which shares to which it relates were delivered to the company

Shares were purchased by the company under section 162 of the above Act as follows:

Class of shares			
Number of shares purchased			
Nominal value of each share			
Date(s) on which the shares were delivered to the company			
Maximum prices paid § for each share			
Minimum prices paid § for each share			

§ A private company is not required to give this information

The aggregate amount paid by the company for the shares to which this return relates was:	£
Stamp duty payable pursuant to section 66 of the Finance Act 1986 on the aggregate amount at 50p per £100 or part of £100	£

‡ Insert Director, Secretary, Receiver, Administrator, Administrative Receiver or Receiver (Scotland) as appropriate

Signed   Designation‡   Date

Presentor's name address and reference (if any):

For official Use
General Section   Post room

Figure A3.5   Return by a company purchasing its own shares

G

COMPANIES FORM No.173

**Declaration in relation to
the redemption or purchase
of shares out of capital**

173

Please do not
write in
this margin

Pursuant to section 173 of the Companies Act 1985

Please complete
legibly, preferably
in black type, or
bold block lettering

To the Registrar of Companies
(Address overleaf - Note 4)

Name of company

For official use   Company number

* insert full name
of company

Note
Please read the notes
on page 2 before
completing this form.

ø insert name(s) and
address(es) of all
the directors

I/We ø _____

_____

_____

_____

_____

_____

_____

_____

† delete as
appropriate

[the sole director][all the directors]† of the above company do solemnly and sincerely declare that:

The business of the company is:

§ delete whichever
is inappropriate

(a) that of a [recognised bank][licensed institution]† within the meaning of the Banking Act 1979§

(b) that of a person authorised under section 3 or 4 of the Insurance Companies Act 1982 to carry on

insurance business in the United Kingdom§

(c) that of something other than the above§

The company is proposing to make a payment out of capital for the redemption or purchase of its own

shares

The amount of the permissible capital payment for the shares in question is £_____
(note 1)

Continued overleaf

Presentor's name address and
reference (if any):

For official Use
General Section   Post room

Page 1

Figure A3.6   Declaration in relation to the redemption or purchase of
shares out of capital

G

COMPANIES FORM No. 190

Notice of place where a register of holders of debentures or a duplicate is kept or of any change in that place

190

Note: This notice is not required where the register is, and has always been, kept at the Registered Office

Pursuant to section 190 of the Companies Act 1985

Please do not write in this margin

Please complete legibly, preferably in block type, or bold block lettering

To the Registrar of Companies (Address overleaf)

For official use

Company number

* insert full name of company

Name of company

† delete as appropriate

gives notice that [a register][registers]† [in duplicate form]† of holders of debentures of the company of the classes mentioned below[is][are]† now kept at:

Postcode

Brief description of class of debentures

‡ Insert Director, Secretary, Administrator, Administrative Receiver or Receiver (Scotland) as appropriate

Signed

Designation‡

Date

Presentor's name address and reference (if any):

For official Use

General Section

Post room

Figure A3.7 Notice of place where a register of holders of debentures or a duplicate is kept or of any change in that place

COMPANIES HOUSE

*Please complete in typescript,
or in bold black capitals.*

325

Location of register of directors' interests in shares etc.

Company Number

Company Name in full

*F 3 2 5 0 0 1 0 *

The register of directors' interests in shares and/or debentures is kept at:

NOTE:
The register MUST be
kept at an address in
the country of
incorporation.

This notice is not
required where the
register is and has
always been kept at the
Registered Office.

Address

Post town

County / Region

Postcode

Signed

Date

† Please delete as appropriate.

† a director / secretary / administrator / administrative receiver / receiver manager / receiver

Please give the name, address,
telephone number and, if available,
a DX number and Exchange of
the person Companies House should
contact if there is any query.

Tel

DX number   DX exchange

Companies House receipt date barcode

When you have completed and signed the form please send it to the
Registrar of Companies at:
Companies House, Crown Way, Cardiff, CF4 3UZ   DX 33050 Cardiff
for companies registered in England and Wales
or
Companies House, 37 Castle Terrace, Edinburgh, EH1 2EB
for companies registered in Scotland   **DX 235 Edinburgh**

Form revised March 1995

Figure A3.8   Location of register of directors' interests in shares, etc

G

COMPANIES FORM No.325a

Notice of place for inspection of a register of directors' interests in shares etc. which is kept in a non-legible form, or of any change in that place

325a

Pursuant to the Companies (Registers and Other Records) Regulations 1985

Note:For use only when the register is kept by computer or in some other non-legible form

Please do not write in this margin

Please complete legibly, preferably in block type, or bold block lettering

To the Registrar of Companies
(Address overleaf)

For official use

Company number

Name of company

* insert full name of company

gives notice, in accordance with regulation 3(1) of the Companies (Registers and Other Records) Regulations 1985, that the place for inspection of the register of directors' interests in shares and/or debentures which the company keeps in a non-legible form is [now]†:

† delete as appropriate

Postcode

Signed

[Director][Secretary]† Date

Presentor's name address and reference (if any):

For official Use

General Section

Post room

Figure A3.9   Notice of place for inspection of a register of directors' interests in shares, etc, which is kept in a non-legible form, or of any change in that place

G

COMPANIES FORM No.353a

**Notice of place for inspection of
a register of members which is
kept in a non-legible form,
or of any change in that place**

353a

Please do not
write in
this margin

Pursuant to the Companies (Registers and Other Records) Regulations 1985

Note: For use only when the register is kept by computer or in some other non-legible form

Please complete
legibly, preferably
in black type, or
bold block lettering

To the Registrar of Companies
(Address overleaf)

Name of company

For official use

Company number

* insert full name
of company

*

gives notice, in accordance with regulation 3(1) of the Companies (Registers and Other Records)

Regulations 1985, that the place for inspection of the register of members of the company which the

† delete as
appropriate

company keeps in a non-legible form is [now]†:

Postcode

Signed

[Director][Secretary]† Date

Presentor's name address and
reference (if any):

For official Use
General Section

Post room

Figure A3.10   Notice of place for inspection of a register of members
which is kept in a non-legible form, or of any change in that place

M

COMPANIES FORM No. 397a

**Particulars of an issue of
secured debentures in a series**

397a

Pursuant to section 397 of the Companies Act 1985

Please complete
legibly, preferably
in black type, or
bold block lettering

To the Registrar of Companies
(Address overleaf - Note 3)

For official use

Company number

Name of company

* insert full name
of company

*

Note

Please read notes
overleaf before
completing this form

Date of present issue

Amount of present issue

Particulars as to commission, allowance or discount (note 2)

† delete as
appropriate

Signed _____ Date _____

On behalf of [company][mortgagee/chargee]†

Presentor's name address and
reference (if any):

For official Use

Mortgage Section

Post room

Time Critical Reference

Figure A3.11   Particulars of an issue of secured debentures in a series

M

CHWP000

COMPANIES FORM No. 403a

**Declaration of satisfaction
in full or in part
of mortgage or charge**

403a

Please do not write in this margin

Pursuant to section 403(1) of the Companies Act 1985

Please complete legibly, preferably in black type, or bold block lettering

To the Registrar of Companies
(Address overleaf)

For official use

Company number

Name of company

* insert full name of company

*

I, _____

of _____

† delete as appropriate

[a director][the secretary][the administrator][the administrative receiver]† of the above company, do

solemnly and sincerely declare that the debt for which the charge described below was given has been

insert a description of the instrument(s) creating or evidencing the charge, eg "Mortgage", 'Charge', 'Debenture' etc

paid or satisfied in **[full][part]**†

Date and description of charge # _____

Date of registration ø _____

ø the date of registration may be confirmed from the certificate

Name and address of [chargee][trustee for the debenture holders]† _____

_____

Short particulars of property charged § _____

§ insert brief details of property

_____

And I make this solemn declaration conscientiously believing the same to be true and by virtue of the

provisions of the Statutory Declarations Act 1835.

Declared at _____   Declarant to sign below

_____

| | Day | Month | Year |
| on | | | |

before me _____

A Commissioner for Oaths or Notary Public or Justice of
the Peace or a Solicitor having the powers conferred on a
Commissioner for Oaths.

Presentor's name address and
reference (if any) :

For official Use (02/00)
Mortgage Section   Post room

Figure A3.12   Declaration of satisfaction in full or in part of mortgage or charge

M

CHWP000

COMPANIES FORM No. 403b

Declaration that part of the property or undertaking charged (a) has been released from the charge; (b) no longer forms part of the company's property or undertaking

403b

Please do not write in this margin

Pursuant to section 403(1) (b) of the Companies Act 1985

Please complete legibly, preferably in black type, or bold block lettering

To the Registrar of Companies **(Address overleaf)**

For official use

Company number

Name of company

* insert full name of company

*

I, _____

of _____

† delete as appropriate

[a director][the secretary][the administrator][the administrative receiver]† of the above company, do solemnly and sincerely declare that with respect to the charge described below the part of the property or undertaking described [has been released from the charge][has ceased to form part of the company's property or undertaking]†

insert a description of the instrument(s) creating or evidencing the charge, eg 'Mortgage', 'Charge', 'Debenture' etc

Date and description of charge # _____

ø the date of registration may be confirmed from the certificate

Date of registration ø _____

Name and address of [chargee][trustee for the debenture holders]† _____

§ insert brief details of property or undertaking no longer subject to the charge

Short particulars of property or undertaking released or no longer part of the company's property or undertaking § _____

_____

And I make this solemn declaration conscientiously believing the same to be true and by virtue of the provisions of the Statutory Declarations Act 1835.

Declared at _____   Declarant to sign below

_____

| | Day | Month | Year |
on | | | |

before me _____

A Commissioner for Oaths or Notary Public or Justice of the Peace or a Solicitor having the powers conferred on a Commissioner for Oaths.

Presentor's name address and reference (if any) :

For official Use (02/00)
Mortgage Section

Post room

Figure A3.13   Declaration that part of the property or undertaking charged (a) has been released from the charge; (b) no longer forms part of the company's property or undertaking

M
CHWP000

COMPANIES FORM No. 466(Scot)

**Particulars of an instrument of
alteration to a floating charge created
by a company registered in Scotland**

466

**A fee of £10 is payable to Companies House in respect
of each register entry for a mortgage or charge.**

*Please do not
write in
this margin*

Pursuant to section 410 and 466 of the Companies Act 1985

**Please complete
legibly, preferably
in black type, or
bold block lettering**

To the Registrar of Companies
(Address overleaf - Note 6)

For official use

Company number

Name of company

** insert full name
of company*

*

Date of creation of the charge (note 1)

Description of the instrument creating or evidencing the charge or of any ancillary document which has
been altered (note 1)

Names of the persons entitled to the charge

Short particulars of all the property charged

Presentor's name address and
reference (if any):

For official use
Charges Section

Post room

Page 1

Figure A3.14   Particulars of an instrument of alteration to a floating
charge created by a company registered in Scotland

M

CHWP000

COMPANIES FORM No. 419a(Scot)

Application for registration of a memorandum of satisfaction in full or in part of a registered charge

419a

Please do not write in this margin

Pursuant to section 419(1) (a) of the Companies Act 1985

Please complete legibly, preferably in black type, or bold block lettering

To the Registrar of Companies
(Address overleaf)

For official use

Company number

Name of company

* insert full name of company

*

I, _____

of _____

[a director] [the secretary] [the liquidator] [the receiver] [the administrator]† of the company,

do solemnly and sincerely declare that the debt for which the charge described overleaf was given has been paid or satisfied in **[full] [part]**†

And I make this solemn declaration conscientiously believing the same to be true and by virtue of the provisions of the Statutory Declarations Act 1835.

† delete as appropriate

Declared at _____   Declarant sign below

_____

_____

| | Day | Month | Year |

on [ ]

before me _____

A Commissioner for Oaths or Notary Public or Justice of the Peace or Solicitor having the powers conferred on a Commissioner for Oaths

Presentor's name address and reference (if any):

For official use

Charges Section

Post room

Page 1

Figure A3.15   Application for registration of a memorandum of satisfaction in full or in part of a registered charge

M

CHWP000

Please do not write in this margin

Please complete legibly, preferably in black type, or bold block lettering

* insert full name of company

† *delete as appropriate*

COMPANIES FORM No. 419b(Scot)

Application for registration of a memorandum of fact that part of the property charged (a) has been released from the charge; (b) no longer forms part of the company's property

419b

Pursuant to section 419(1) (b) of the Companies Act 1985

To the Registrar of Companies
(Address overleaf)

For official use

Company number

Name of company

*

I, _____

of _____

[a director] [the secretary] [the liquidator] [the receiver] [the administrator]† of the company, do solemnly and
sincerely declare that the particulars overleaf relating to the charge and the fact that part of the property or
undertaking charged [ceased to form part of the company's property or undertaking] [was released from the
charge]† on _____ are
true to the best of my knowledge and belief.

And I make this solemn declaration conscientiously believing the same to be true and by virtue of the
provisions of the Statutory Declarations Act 1835.

Declared at _____   Declarant sign below

_____

_____

Day   Month   Year

on

before me _____

A Commissioner for Oaths or Notary Public or Justice of
the Peace or Solicitor having the powers conferred on a
Commissioner for Oaths

Presentor's name address and
reference (if any):

For official use
Charges Section   Post room

Page 1

Figure A3.16   Application for registration of a memorandum of fact that part of the property charged (a) has been released from the charge; (b) no longer forms part of the company's property

Appendix 4

Books, registers and documents which must be available for inspection and of which copies or extracts can be requisitioned

Book etc	Who can inspect	Fee	Who can requisition	Time limit for sending	Penalty
Memorandum and Articles	-	-	Any member	Not specified	£400 (company and each officer in default)
Annual Accounts, ie auditors' report, directors' report, balance sheet and profit and loss account	Copy to all members, debenture holders	None	Members and debenture holders	7 days	Unlimited fine on conviction on indictment, £2,000 + £200 daily on summary conviction or £400 + £40 daily (company and each officer in default)

*To be kept at the registered office or at such other place as the directors designate.
**To be kept at the registered office.

Book etc	Who can inspect	Fee	Who can requisition	Time limit for sending	Penalty
*Accounting records	Officers at all times	None	–	--	On indictment 2 years' prison and/or fine; summary conviction 6 months' prison and/or £2,000 fine+ £200 daily
Book, vouchers accounts	Auditors at all times	None	–	–	–
	Liquidator	–	–	–	On indictment 7 years' prison and/ or fine; summary conviction 6 months' prison and/or £2,000 fine+ £200 daily
**Charge requiring registration, copy of instrument	Members and creditors	None	–	–	£400 + £40 daily
Directors' service contracts, copies, or notes of their contents	Members	None	–	–	ditto
**Minute book general meeting	Members	None	Members	–	7 days £400; court can make order

Book etc	Who can inspect	Fee	Who can requisition	Time limit for sending	Penalty
**Register of charges	Members, creditors, Anyone else	None Not exceeding 5p	–	–	£400 + fine £40 daily; court can make order
*Register of debenture holders	Members, debenture holders Anyone else	None Not exceeding 5p	Anyone	–	ditto
*Register of directors and secretaries	Members Anyone else	None Not exceeding 5p	–	–	£2,000 fine+ £200 daily
**Register of directors' interests	Members Anyone else	None Not exceeding 5p	Anyone	10 days	£400 + £40 daily
**Register of members and index	Members Anyone else	None Not exceeding 5p	Members anyone else	Within 10 days of day after receipt of request	£400, court can make order
Special resolution	–	–	Members	Not specified	£400
Extraordinary resolution	–	–	ditto	ditto	ditto
Members' resolution	–	–	ditto	ditto	ditto
Resolution for winding up	–	–	Members	ditto	ditto
Trust deed securing debenture	–	–	Debenture holders	ditto	£400 + £40 daily

Notes:
1. Penalties: Both the company and its officers can be liable for fines.
2. Memorandum: If the Memorandum is altered, the company and officers in default are liable to a fine of £200 in respect of each copy subsequently issued without the amendment.
3. Accounting Records: Officers in default have a defence if they acted honestly and the default was excusable in the circumstances, but the records must be retained for at least three years.
4. Books, vouchers and accounts: If records are inadequate or access is denied, this must be stated in the auditors' report.
5. Charges requiring registration: The instrument must be available for inspection during business hours, subject to reasonable restrictions imposed by the company in general meeting, but it must be accessible for at least two hours daily.
6. Directors' service contracts etc, the Minute book, the Register of charges, Register of debenture holders and the Register of directors and secretaries: These must be available on the same basis and the Register of directors' interests must in addition be produced at the Annual General Meeting and remain open and accessible throughout; the Register of members can, however, be closed for not more than 30 days a year, provided notice of closure is advertised in a newspaper local to the registered office.
7. Special resolution and a Resolution for winding up: If the Articles are not registered, a printed copy of the resolution must be filed. If they are registered, the resolution must be annexed to or incorporated in every copy of the Articles issued.

Appendix 5

Useful notices and notes

XYZ Limited

Notice is hereby given that the First **Annual General Meeting** of the Company will be held on___day the___day of___20__ at__o'clock in the fore/after noon to transact the following business:

To receive and adopt the Accounts of the Company for the year ended____ together with the Reports of the Directors and the Auditors.

To declare a dividend.

To re-appoint/appoint_____as Auditors of the Company.

To fix the remuneration of the Auditors and to transact any other business which may lawfully be transacted at an Annual General Meeting.

A member entitled to attend and vote at the above meeting may appoint a proxy to attend and vote in his stead. A proxy need not be a member of the company.

By order of the Board

Signed_____

Secretary

Figure A5.1   Notice of Annual General Meeting

XYZ Limited

Notice is hereby given that an **Extraordinary General Meeting** of the above named Company will be held at_____ on _____day the _____day of _____20___ at ____o'clock in the fore/after noon for the purpose of considering and if thought fit passing the Resolution set out below which will be proposed as an Ordinary/Special/Extraordinary Resolution.

A member entitled to attend and vote at the above meeting may appoint a proxy to attend and on a poll* vote in his stead. A proxy need not be a member of the company.

By order of the Board

Signed _____
Secretary

Resolution

*If the Articles permit a proxy to vote on a show of hands, delete the words 'on a poll'.

Figure A5.2   Notice of meeting

Company number _____

Company name _____

At an **Extraordinary General*/Annual General*/General* Meeting** of the members of the above named Company duly convened and held at:

_____

_____

on the_____day of _____ 20___

the following **Special Resolution** was duly passed:

That the name of the Company be changed to:

(new name) _____

Signature: _____ Chairman, Director, Secretary or Officer of the Company

NB. A copy of the Resolution must be filed with the Registrar within 15 days after the passing of the Resolution.

*Delete as appropriate

Figure A5.3   Special resolution on change of name

Company number _____

Company name _____

We, the undersigned, being all the members of the above Company for the time being entitled to receive notice of, attend and vote at General Meetings, hereby unanimously pass the following resolution and agree that the said resolution shall pass for all purposes be as valid and effective as if the same had been passed at a General Meeting of the Company duly convened and held at:

It is resolved that:

Dated this_____day of _____ 20___

Signed: _____

_____

_____

_____

Figure A5.4   Written resolution

AGREEMENT of MEMBERS to SHORT NOTICE of a GENERAL MEETING and/or of a SPECIAL RESOLUTION

(1) 'I' or 'WE'.
(2) 'Annual' or 'Extraordinary' as the case may be.

(1) _____ the undersigned, being member of the above-named Company and entitled to attend and vote (2) _____ General Meeting of the said Company convened by a Notice of Meeting dated the _____ day of _____ 20 _____ and to be held on the _____ day of _____ 20 _____ , hereby agree that:

1.* The said meeting shall be deemed to have been duly called, notwithstanding that shorter notice than that specified in section 369 of the Companies Act 1985, or in the Company's Articles of Association, has been given therefor.

2.* The copies of the documents referred to in sections 239 and 240 of the Companies Act 1985, which were attached to or enclosed with the said Notice of Meeting, shall be deemed to have been duly sent, notwithstanding that such copies were sent less than twenty-one days before the date of the meeting.

3. The Special Resolution set out in the said Notice of Meeting may be proposed and passed as Special Resolution notwithstanding that such less than twenty-one days' notice of such meeting has been given.

NAME (in block capitals)	ADDRESS	SIGNATURE†

NOTES

* Delete this paragraph if not required.

† The documents referred to are the company's profit and loss account and balance sheet, the directors' report, the auditors' report and, where the Company has subsidiaries and section 229 applies, the Company's group accounts.

‡(a) In the case where agreement is required only to the holding of an Extraordinary General Meeting, and/or to the passing of Special Resolutions at an Extraordinary General Meeting, on short notice, agreement must be given by a majority in number of the members having a right to attend and vote at the meeting, being a majority together holding not less than 95 per cent in nominal value of the shares giving a right to attend and vote at the meeting, or, in the case of a company not having a share capital, together representing not less than 95 per cent of the total voting rights at the meeting of all the members.

(b) In any other case, agreement must be given by all the members entitled to attend and vote at the meeting.

(c) One form may be signed by all the members concerned, or several similar forms may be signed by one or more of them.

Figure A5.5 Agreements of members to short notice of a general meeting and/or of a special resolution

Section 369 (3) and *(4)* of the Companies Act 1985 provide as follows:

(3) Notwithstanding that a meeting is called by shorter notice than that specified in subsection (2) or in the company's articles (as the case may be), it is deemed to have been duly called if it is so agreed:

    (a) in the case of a meeting called as the annual general meeting, by all the members entitled to attend and vote at it; and

    (b) otherwise, by the requisite majority.

(4) The requisite majority for this purpose is a majority in number of the members having a right to attend and vote at the meeting, being a majority:

    (a) together holding not less than 95 per cent in nominal value of the shares giving a right to attend and vote at the meeting; or

    (b) in the case of a company not having a share capital, together representing not less than 95 per cent of the total voting rights at that meeting of all the members.

Section 378 (2) and *(3)* of the Companies Act 1985 provide as follows:

(2) A resolution is a special resolution when it has been passed by such a majority as is required for the passing of an extraordinary resolution and at a general meeting of which not less than 21 days' notice, specifying the intention to propose the resolution as a special resolution, has been duly given.

(3) If it is so agreed by a majority in number of the members having the right to attend and vote at such a meeting, being a majority:

    (a) together holding not less than 95 per cent in nominal value of the shares giving that right; or

    (b) in the case of a company not having a share capital, together representing not less than 95 per cent of the total voting rights at that meeting of all the members,

a resolution may be proposed and passed as a special resolution at a meeting of which less than 21 days' notice has been given.

Section 239 of the Companies Act 1985 provides as follows:

For the purposes of this Part, a company's accounts for a financial year are to be taken as comprising the following documents:

    (a) the company's profit and loss account and balance sheet,

    (b) the directors' report,

    (c) the auditors' report, and

    (d) where the company has subsidiaries and section 229 applies, the company's group accounts.

Section 240 of the Companies Act 1985 provides as follows:

(1) In the case of every company, a copy of the company's accounts for the financial year shall, not less than 21 days before the date of the meeting at which

they are to be laid in accordance with the next section, be sent to each of the following persons:

(*a*) every member of the company (whether or not entitled to receive notice of general meetings),

(*b*) every holder of the company's debenture (whether or not so entitled), and

(*c*) all persons other than members and debenture holders, being persons so entitled.

(2) In the case of a company not having a share capital, subsection (1) does not require a copy of the accounts to be sent to a member of the company who is not entitled to receive notices of general meetings of the company, or to a holder of the company's debentures who is not so entitled.

(3) Subsection (1) does not require copies of the accounts to be sent:

(*a*) to a member of the company or a debenture holder, being in either case a person who is not entitled to receive notices of general meetings, and of whose address the company is unaware, or

(*b*) to more than one of the joint holders of any shares or debentures none of whom are entitled to receive such notices, or

(*c*) in the case of joint holders of shares or debentures some of whom are, and some not, entitled to receive such notices, to those who are not so entitled.

(4) If copies of the accounts are sent less than 21 days before the date of the meeting, they are, notwithstanding that fact, deemed to have been duly sent if it is so agreed by all the members entitled to attend and vote at the meeting.

Obligation to print certain documents

The Companies Act 1985

The European Communities Act 1972

1. The following documents are required to be printed:
   (a) Articles of Association
   (b) Altered Memorandums of Association
   (c) Altered Articles of Association
2. The Registrar of Companies is prepared to regard the printing stipulation as satisfied by the following processes:
   Letterpress, Gravure, Lithography.
   Stencil duplicating, Offset lithography, 'Office' typeset.
   Electrostatic photocopying.
   'Photostat' or similar processes properly processed and washed.
   Stencil duplicating, using wax stencils and black ink.

3. The following documents when submitted for registration must be either printed or in a form approved by the Registrar:
    (a) Ordinary Resolutions increasing the capital of any company.
    (b) Special and Extraordinary Resolutions and Agreements as specified in section 380 of the Companies Act 1985.
    The Registrar is prepared to accept for registration such copy Resolutions and Agreements if produced by a process named in paragraph 2 above or by spirit duplicator, of if typed.

4. No document will be accepted if it is illegible. Where it is considered that a document, though legible, cannot be reproduced to an adequate standard for presentation to the public in microfiche or photocopy form, the Registrar's practice is to seek the cooperation of the presentor in providing a clearer copy.

5. The Registrar's present practice is to accept copies of the Memorandum and Articles amended in accordance with the following rules:
    Where the amendment is small in extent, eg a change of name or a change in the nominal capital, a copy of the original document may be amended by rubber stamp, 'top copy' typing or in some other permanent manner (but not a manuscript amendment).
    An alteration of a few lines or a complete short paragraph may be similarly dealt with if the new version is satisfactorily permanently affixed to a copy of the original in such a way as to obscure the amended words.
    Where more substantial amendments are involved, the pages amended may be removed from a copy of the original, the amended text inserted and the pages securely collated. The inserted material must be 'printed' as defined above but need not be produced by the same process as the original.
    In all cases the alterations must be validated by the seal or an official stamp of the company.

6. Where the document is produced other than by letterpress, a certificate by the printer stating the process used must be endorsed on or accompany the document.

7. It has been found the experience that documents produced by semi-dry developed dye line (diazo) copies produced by spirit duplicating or thermo-copying do not satisfy the general conditions.

COMPANIES ACTS

Elective Resolution
(Pursuant to section 379A of the Companies Act 1985)

Company number _____

Company name _____

At an Extraordinary General Meeting of the above-named company duly convened and held at:

_____

_____

on the_____day of _____ 20___

the following Elective Resolution was duly passed:

It is resolved that:

Signed: _____

NOTE: to be filed within 15 days of passing the Resolution.

Figure A5.6   Elective resolution

Section 379A of the Companies Act 1985 provides as follows:

(1) An election by a private company for the purposes of:
   (a) section 80A (election as to duration of authority to allot shares);
   (b) section 252 (election to dispense with laying of accounts and reports before general meeting);
   (c) section 366A (election to dispense with holding of annual general meeting);
   (d) section 369 (4) or 378 (3) (election as to majority required to authorise short notice of meeting);
or
   (e) section 386 (election to dispense with appointment of auditors annually), shall be made by resolution of the company in general meeting in accordance with this section. Such a resolution is referred to in this Act as an 'elective resolution'.

(2) An elective resolution is not effective unless:
   (a) at least 21 days' notice in writing is given of the meeting, stating that an elective resolution is to be proposed and stating the terms of the resolution; and
   (b) the resolution is agreed to at the meeting, in person or by proxy, by all the members entitled to attend and vote at the meeting.

(3) The company may revoke an elective resolution by passing an ordinary resolution to that effect.

(4) An elective resolution shall cease to have effect if the company is re-registered as a public company.

(5) An elective resolution may be passed or revoked in accordance with this section and the provisions referred to in subsection (1) have effect notwithstanding any contrary provision in the company's Articles of Association.

NOTE: The Registrar of Companies is prepared to accept copy resolutions or agreements if produced to a standard which is legible and can be reproduced to an adequate standard for presentation to the public in microfiche or photocopied format. Signatures must, however, be original and not photocopied.

Widgets Limited

I, _____ of _____

being a member of the above named Company and entitled to vote

hereby appoint _____ of _____

or him failing _____ of _____

as my proxy to attend and vote for me and on my behalf at the
Annual/Extraordinary General Meeting of the Company to be held

on _____ day the _____ day of _____ Two thousand

and _____, and at any adjournment thereof

As witness My hand this _____ day of _____ 20____

Signed _____

in the presence of _____ *

This proxy must be deposited at the Registered Office of the
Company not less than _____ hours before the time fixed for
holding the above mentioned meeting

NB. Any alterations made to the form must be initialled by the
signatory and the witness

*If the Company's Articles require the signature to be witnessed, the
witness should write in his name, address and occupation.

Figure A5.7   Form of proxy

Appendix 6

Useful addresses

Association of Company Registration Agents
20 Holywell Row
London EC2A 4XH
Tel: 020 7377 0381

British Chambers of Commerce
Manning House
22 Carlisle Place
London SW1P 1JA
Tel: 020 7565 2000
Web site: www.britishchambers.org.uk

British Insurance Brokers Association
BIBA House
14 Bevis Marks
London EC3A 7NT
Tel: 020 7623 9043
Web site: www.biba.org.uk

Business Angels
National Business Angels Network
40–42 Cannon Street
London EC4N 6JJ
Tel: 020 7329 2929
Web site: www.nationalbusangels.co.uk

Business Link
National Contact Centre: 0845 600 9006
Web site: www.businesslink.org
(There are also numerous local Business Links.)

Capital Taxes Office England and Wales
Ferrers House
PO Box 38
Castle Meadow Road
Nottingham NG2 1BB
Tel: 0115 974 2400
Web site: www.inlandrevenue.gov.uk.cto

Northern Ireland
Level 3, Dorchester House
52–58 Great Victoria Street
Belfast BT2 7QL
Tel: 028 9050 5353

Scotland
Meldrum House
15 Drumshengh Gardens
Edinburgh EH3 7UG
Tel: 0131 777 4050

Central Office of Information
Hercules House
Hercules Road
London SE1 7DU
Tel: 020 7928 2345
Web site: coi.gov.uk

Chartered Association of Certified Accountants
29 Lincoln's Inn Fields
London WC2A 3EE
Tel: 020 7396 5800
Web site: www.accaglobal.com

Chartered Institute of Arbitrators
12 Bloomsbury Square
London WC1A 2LP
Tel: 020 7421 7444
Web site: www.arbritrators.org

Chartered Institute of Management Accountants
63 Portland Place
London W1N 4AB
Tel: 020 7917 9277
Web site: www.cimaglobal.com

Companies House

The telephone number for all branches is: 0870 33 33 363

Cardiff:
Crown Way
Maindy Cardiff CF14 3UZ

London:
21 Bloomsbury Street
London WC1B 32XD

Birmingham:
Central Library
Chamberlain Square
Birmingham B3 3HQ

Leeds:
25 Queen Street
Leeds LS1 2TW

Manchester:
75 Mosley Street
Manchester M2 3HR

Edinburgh:
37 Castle Terrace
Edinburgh EH1 2EB

Competition Commission, The
New Court
48 Carey Street
London WC2A 2JT
Tel: 020 7271 0100
Web site: www.competition-commission.gov.uk

Confederation of British Industry (CBI)
Centre Point
New Oxford Street
London WC1A 1DU
Tel: 020 7379 7400

Consumer Credit Trade Association
Suite 8
The Wool Exchange
10 Hustlergate
Bradford BD1 1RE
Tel: 01274 390380

Customs and Excise
New King's Beam House
22 Upper Ground
London SE1 9PJ
Tel: 020 7620 1313

Data Protection Registration Office
Springfield House
Water Lane
Wilmslow
Cheshire SK9 5AX
Tel: 01625 535777

Department for Education and Skills
The Sanctuary Buildings
Great Smith Street
London SW1P 3BT
Tel: 0870 000 2288
E-mail: info@dfes.gsi.gov.uk
Web site: www.dfes.gov.uk

Department of Trade and Industry
1 Victoria Street
London SW1H 0ET
Tel: 020 7215 5000
Web site: www.dti.gov.uk

European Patent Office
Erhardtstrasse 27 8033
Munich
Germany
Tel: 4989 23990
Web site: www.european-patent-office.org

Export Credits Guarantee Department
2 Exchange Tower
PO Box 2200
Harbour Exchange Square
London E14 9GS
Tel: 020 7512 7000
Web site: www.ecgd.gov.uk

Finance and Leasing Association
15–19 Kingsway
London WC2B 6UN
Tel: 020 7836 6511
Web site: www.fla.org.uk

Inland Revenue
Tel: 020 7438 6420

Public Enquiry Room
Bush House
The Strand
London WC2

Superannuation Funds Office
York House
PO Box 62
Nottingham NG2 1BG
Tel: 0115 974 1600

Profit Related Pay Office
St Mungo's Road
Cumbernauld
Glasgow G70 5TR
Tel: 01236 736121

Institute of Chartered Accountants in England and Wales
PO Box 433
Moorgate Place
London EC2P 2BJ
Tel: 020 7920 8100

Institute of Chartered Accountants in Ireland
87–89 Pembroke Road
Dublin 4
Republic of Ireland
Tel: 00 3531 637 7200

11 Donegall Square South
Belfast BT1 5JE
Northern Ireland
Tel: 028 9032 1600

Institute of Chartered Accountants of Scotland
CA House
21 Haymarket Yards
Edinburgh EH12 5BH
Tel: 0131 347 0100
Web site: www.icas.org.uk

Institute of Chartered Secretaries and Administrators
16 Park Crescent
London W1N 4AH
Tel: 020 7580 4741
Web site: www.icsa.org.uk

Institute of Directors
116 Pall Mall
London SW1Y 5ED
Tel: 020 7839 1233
Web site: www.iod.com

Institute of Management
Management House
Cottingham Road
Corby
Northamptonshire NN17 1TT
Tel: 01536 204222
Web site: www.inst.mgt.org.uk

Insurance Ombudsman Bureau
The Financial Ombudsman Service
South Quay Plaza
183 Marsh Wall
London E14 9SR
Tel: 0845 080 1800
Web site: www.theiob.org.uk

International Chamber of Commerce
14–15 Belgrave Square
London SW1X 8PS
Tel: 020 7823 2811

Land Charges Registry
The Superintendent Land Charges Department
DX 8249
Plumer House
Tailyour Road
Crownhill
Plymouth PL6 5HY
Tel: 01752 635600
Web site: landreg.gov.uk
(There are 24 Land Registries in England and Wales)

Law Society, The
113 Chancery Lane
London WC2A 1PL
Tel: 020 7242 1222
Web site: www.lawsociety.org.uk

Learning and Skills Council
Cheylesmore House
Quinton Road
Coventry CV1 2WT
Tel: 0845 019 4170
Web site: www.lsc.gov.uk

London Chamber of Commerce
33 Queen Street
London EC4R 1AD
Tel: 020 7248 4444
Web site: www.londonchamber.co.uk
(Business Registry offers free advice and search facilities to members)

London Gazette
PO Box 7923
London SE1 5ZH
Tel: 020 7394 4580
Web site: www.london-gazette.co.uk

Office of Fair Trading
Fleetbank House
2-6 Salisbury Square
London EC4Y 8JX
Tel: 020 7211 8000
Web site: www.oft.gov.uk

The Patent Office
Concept House
Cardiff Road
Newport
South Wales NP10 8QQ
Tel: 08459 500 505
Web site: www.patent.gov.uk

Registry of County Court Judgments
171–173 Cleveland Street
London W1P 5PE
Tel: 020 7380 0133

The Stationery Office/Her Majesty's Stationery Office (HMSO)
St Crispins
Duke Street
Norwich NR3 1PD
Tel: 0870 600 5522
Web sites: www.thestationeryoffice.com or www.hmso.gov.uk

Trade Marks Registry
The Patent Office
Cardiff Road
Newport
Gwent NP9 1RH
Tel: 01633 814000

Leading formations' agents

4 Business Limited
72 New Bond Street
London W1S 1RR
Tel: 020 7514 9904
Web site: www.4business.com

A1 Company Services Limited
788–790 Finchley Road
London NW11 7TJ
Tel: 0202 8458 9637
Web site: www.a1companies.com

Jordans Limited
21 St Thomas Street
Bristol BS1 6JS
Tel: 0117 923 0600
Web site: www.jordans.co.uk

The London Law Agency Limited
69 Southampton Row
London WC1B 4ET
Tel: 0800 174 458
Web site: www.londonlaw.co.uk

SDG (Stanley Davis Group)
120 East Road
London N1 6AA
Tel: 020 7253 0800
Web site: www.sdgonline.com

York Place Company Services Limited
12 York Place
Leeds LS1 2DS
Tel: 0113 242 0222
Web site: www.yorkplace.co.uk

Waterlow Legal & Company Services
6–8 Underwood Street
London N1 7JQ
Tel: 020 7250 3350
Web site: www.waterlow.com

Index

Index of advertisers